# *Advance Praise*

"It is very rare to find a seasoned security, risk, and privacy executive who can successfully combine storytelling, historic military leadership analogies, and technology and management challenges into a very compelling, readable, and relevant reference book that reads like a novel. Most importantly, rather than teaching the reader how to "do" security, privacy, and risk management, Nick describes how to "think" about it and stay in front of the challenges and ever-changing landscape... the psychology of security, privacy, and risk management, if you will. A must-have book for those interested in how to gain awareness of the digital threat landscape and continually strategize defensives relevant to both the business and technology within their organization."

— DR. JAMES RANSOME, CISSP, CISM,
VETERAN CISO, CPSO, AND AUTHOR

"Applying the wisdom of the sages of military strategy to IT in general and to security in particular is long overdue. Nick's tangible passion for the topic illuminates issues he and every contemporary CISO confront on a daily basis. The insights are extremely timely in that CISOs are now confronting an attack space generated by work-from-home jobs where the exposure has exponentially increased. Going forward, ubiquitous edge computing connected by low-latency XG will create yet another dimension of vulnerability. While technology can provide some of the solution with zero trust as the mantra, the savvy CISO understands well its perils.

"The book begins with a personal memoir of Nick's childhood exposure to the dark side. As any VC will attest, firsthand experience of pain is an essential foundation for innovation. Forged in this cauldron, Nick cleverly applies the fundamental principles of military strategy from Sun Tzu to Lee and Grant (with significant contributors in between) to the contemporary nightmares CISOs confront.

"This book is no academic exercise; Nick captures the key tenets of the strategists and their teachings and then pulls them down to actionable practices a CIO/CISO could deploy. This is the hallmark of every chapter. For example, in Chapter Four, he applies the teachings of Sun Tzu and Marcus Aurelius to digital warfare. The depth of context in which Nick illuminates the principles he applies is stunning. As a student of philosophy, I had no idea Zeno, famed for his paradoxes, was a Phoenician merchant who fermented oysters to extract purple dye used for royal garments. This and other insights make *Cyber War...and Peace* a captivating read as well as a playbook for the contemporary CISO and CIO. Some of the stories will elevate the boardroom discussions these modern warriors confront.

"As a student of the topic, Napoleon's strategy at Austerlitz continues to be a quintessential lesson in dynamic strategies. How to apply it to modern-day security is key. Promoting flexibility as the key to managing in a state of constant flux is a fundamental principle. Nick illustrates this with his advice on when to hunker down to be robust and resilient and when to feint and use guile to deceive an adversary, just as Napoleon did with the fog obscuring his Old Guard elite troops to lure his enemies into a trap.

"The book is loaded with templates and exercises. The conclusion provides many checklists as a practical guide for the digital CISO to help them see through the fog of digital warfare. There's help in dealing with questions board members may have concerning cybersecurity too. Taken together, Nick's book is both an intellectual sojourn into the intricacies and lessons we can derive from the sages of military strategy, and yet he has the practical experience to transfer these insights into practical guides. This book is a must for every CISO's top drawer!"

— STUART EVANS, DISTINGUISHED SERVICE PROFESSOR<br>AT CARNEGIE MELLON UNIVERSITY

"As a discipline we need to apply more lessons from the past. Not just the immediate lessons from recent memory but also the well-worn paths across history. Nick does an excellent job of bridging the non-cyber past into our cyber present with practical risk management and leadership guidance for everyone building and evolving an enterprise security program."

— PHIL VENABLES

NICHOLAS SHEVELYOV

# CYBER WAR

# ...AND

# PEACE

## BUILDING DIGITAL TRUST TODAY
## WITH HISTORY AS OUR GUIDE

LIONCREST
PUBLISHING

Cyber War . . . and Peace
Building Digital Trust Today With History As Our Guide

ISBN  978-1-5445-1709-4 *Hardcover*
    978-1-5445-1708-7 *Paperback*
    978-1-5445-1707-0 *Ebook*
    978-1-5445-2210-4 *Audiobook*

# CONTENTS

*To my loving family,
friends, and colleagues who have
influenced me over the years.
You have inspired me to become
a better version of myself.
Thank you.*

WINSTON CHURCHILL ONCE SAID,

"WE MAKE A LIVING OFF OF

WHAT WE GET,

BUT WE MAKE A LIFE BY

WHAT WE GIVE."

*Proceeds from this book will be donated.*

# FOREWORD

## Robert D. Rodriguez,
## Chairman and Founder, SINET

THIS FOREWORD SERVES as an appetizer before the upcoming entree. Nick has authored a personal and philosophical story that masterfully blends historical metaphors with salient points on his journey from the early days of cybersecurity to present-day risk management.

Nick captures the reader's interest from page one, a young boy's memory of driving through downtown Moscow. We quickly learn how his formative years fueled his view of risk and his interest in the field of technology. This is a book designed for business leaders who want to learn more about the increasingly important area of cyber risk management.

Ronald Reagan's management style is ever-present throughout the book: "Surround yourself with the best people you can find, delegate authority, and don't interfere as long as the policy you've decided upon is being carried out." Essentially, put your ego into your pocket.

Numerous anecdotes of legendary icons and figures of Greek mythology highlight their fragility and hubris, weaknesses and strengths. Making oneself vulnerable and walking with humility are keys to success, and Nick addresses this point throughout his book. I, too, have fallen off the high horse, but the key to not repeating one's overconfidence, no matter how successful you are, is to never forget what it feels like to fall.

After reading Nick's book, it is easy to understand why he applied historical nuggets of wisdom from thousands of years ago which are still relevant today. He makes history applicable, interesting, and memorable, as it continues to repeat itself. Part of Nick's message is that we can work smarter and make life better and more productive if we learn from humankind's past mistakes.

I served for twenty-two years as a special agent in the United States Secret Service (USSS) protecting Presidents Reagan, Bush (41), Clinton, and Bush (43)—an extraordinary experience that took me to sixty countries where I was witness to several historical events. These experiences shaped me with a strong sense of mission, integrity, and purpose. Readers who have served in the military or other branches of law enforcement will also relate to the numerous analogies about decisions made by leaders such as Napoleon, Marcus Aurelius, and Sun Tzu.

The logistics for presidential visits required an enormous number of resources and planning to support the visiting advance teams: USSS agents, White House staff, Communications, Countersniper, K-9, Medical, Transportation, Marine One, Air Force One, C-130s, motorcade routes, protective intelligence teams, countersurveillance teams, first responders, Technical Security Division, Counter Assault Team (CAT)—all with their own unique roles and responsibilities. This is not unlike the respective duties of corporate or government security teams in that all have specific roles and responsibilities.

When agents request a certain number of employees and resources, they are invariably told: "You are getting less than requested and that's it, so make it happen." As an agent, this is when you have to evaluate your risk posture and strategically apply your resources to the most vulnerable areas within your perimeter, which, to include the space above and below you, consists of a 360-degree circumference. You conduct numerous assessments, from the number of windows which can or cannot be opened to each manhole cover and what is in it. There are three concentric rings: outer, middle, and inner; the latter for the industry is the family jewels, or, in this case, the President of the United States. This is the last bastion, and there are no options for failure. You plan and plan again, with a back-up to a back-up to a back-up plan. Nick exhibits this same approach throughout his book. Ultimately, the onus is upon every one of us in the business of securing company or government systems. In our own small way, we are all part of a larger and higher calling toward the protection of our nation's critical infrastructures, our national and economic security, our privacy, and our inherent rights as free citizens in a free democracy—it all matters.

Nick outlines numerous philosophies and analogies to lay the framework on how to manage enterprise risk holistically and across all business lines. His alignment of historical scenarios will help readers both understand and remember the principle points in the book.

This is a timely read considering a scenario occurred in 2020 that represented the breach of the century against our national critical infrastructure and federal government.

My time on the president's detail and in particular on CAT helped me understand how to remain calm amidst the human instinct to feel fear and pressure, to measure and listen to the cadence of your breathing during intense situations, to keep your wits about you when others do not so that those you are leading have confidence that you are in control and will ultimately make the right decision.

To Nick, the polymath, the sage, and the boy who nurtured the baby fox, thank you for the opportunity to write this foreword. I am humbled and honored...

# INTRODUCTION

## Catching the Bug

I WAS FIVE years old when my parents told me that our apartment had been bugged.

The United States wasn't a particularly friendly place for Russians when I was born in the 1970s. My parents, both of Russian descent, were born in China, immigrated to the US, met, married, moved to the Pacific Northwest, and eventually gave birth to me. Despite the somewhat hostile environment — or perhaps because of it — they decided they wanted to move back to Russia. There, they hoped to contribute to raising awareness about what life was like in the West in hopes of eroding some of the "iron curtain" that had been drawn up between the East and the West. They also wanted to immerse themselves and their child in the culture of their origin.

My father took a job with the US State Department and we moved to an apartment in Moscow. Although I was only a child, it was quickly clear to me how much our lives had changed. The infrastructure of the Soviet Union was so very different. The architecture was bleak, and the monuments were massive. To this day, I still remember driving from Sheremetyevo Airport in Moscow to our new apartment and being awestruck by the size of the World War II monuments we passed along the way.

Not long after we took up residence in our new apartment, my father learned that our family was being observed by the KGB because they believed us to be spies. After all, we were from America, moving to the Soviet Union at the height of the Cold War, and my father was a retired Marine who worked for the US State Department. Part of this observation meant that we were assigned someone we believed to be a "family friend," a person we met who would join us on excursions to the park, grocery store, and the like. Decades later, we would discover that our family friend was forced by the KGB to report on our movements and develop a dossier about all the things that were said in conversation during the time we spent together. In addition, our apartment had been bugged. My father discovered this fact relatively quickly, though I can't be sure just how he figured it out.

Despite my young age, I remember being very aware of the threat to our security—the idea that at any time the KGB could come and take any one of us away, and that we were constantly being listened to. It created a sort of internal alarm within my family, and we developed new habits as a result. If any of us had something important to say, we would give a hand signal to go into the bathroom, where we would run the faucet as we spoke. The faucet served as white noise to prevent the bugs from picking up any sensitive conversations.

While in the Soviet Union, my father published a book titled *Information Moscow* about the upcoming Olympics, with the goal of attracting Westerners to Russia. In writing this, it was necessary for him to create and utilize an accurate map of Moscow—something the Soviets were none too keen on. One day, not long after publication, a black Lada—the government-issued cars then—arrived at our apartment, and agents took my father away. He was drugged and interrogated about his intentions and who he was working for.

It was then that we all realized the true gravity and absolute precariousness of our situation. We packed up and moved back to the States not long after. We have remained here ever since.

To say that those events in my childhood left an impression on me is an understatement. I saw at a very early age that, at any point in time, someone you love can be taken away from you—that the very sense of your own security and privacy can be fractured and invaded. The experience has, without a doubt, fueled my drive to join the field of technology and contributed to my philosophical view of risk management today.

It also lent to my appetite as a young man for technology and the democratization of data and information. I became fascinated with the idea that we could share information around the world, and that sense of wonder led me to pursue a career in technology.

But in the back of my mind, I also thought about the ways in which information could be misused—used against you, used to do harm—and it steered me toward not just technology, but technology risk management. Or, as we referred to it in the 1990s, IT security.

I started off in network engineering and system administration, but I found myself more drawn to the protection, rather than the creation, of those assets. By the late nineties, my career was focused on information security—breaking into networks (also known as "white hat" operations), hardening them, and protecting the information contained within. I eventually ended up with a security consulting firm that did work for clients, breaking into hardened networks. Eventually, I landed at Deloitte, where I worked for a partner who was also an attorney and who focused on data privacy.

It was my work with him that taught me an important differentiation:

> **Security professionals care about what information you have; they tend to overlook privacy nuances. Privacy professionals, on the other hand, care about how you *use* that information.**

It's that interplay—that balance of identifying information, protecting it, and figuring out how to use it in an enlightened manner—that has laid the foundation and served as the core of my career.

## SPIES LIKE US

THE IRONY IS not lost on me—nor should it be on you—that today, no one has to bug our homes.

The espionage and monitoring game has evolved to a point where it is no longer necessary to have resources assigned to spy on us.

We're spying on ourselves.

We bring into our homes voice-activated devices that we think preserve our privacy. We bring in video surveillance cameras that can be hacked, to the point where the actions within our home can be observed. We update our own dossiers every time we log into social media accounts or check-in at a location on an app.

We consider this the new age of information, but studies suggest it is also an age of disinformation, given that falsified information may spread up to six times faster than fact-based news reporting. Today, surveillance capitalism information exchanges trade in human behavior futures at scale, managed by systems with little human intervention to build models and predict and further influence your behavior.

The reality is that the world is changing more rapidly now than at any point in our history, and that rate of change is continuing to accelerate. We see and feel it every day with the introduction of each new technology service or device that we feel will empower us to do things faster, easier, and more efficiently than the way we did it the month before.

The problem is that we don't spend a lot of—if any—time thinking about how these things introduce risk. Remember, the very technology that empowers us can also imperil us. As such, we bring these devices and technologies into our homes and our organizations without considering how we're letting in the Trojan horse.

This happens in business on a regular basis.

Malicious software known as Trojan horses do this every single day, and they can reap vast amounts of damage to organizations. Some take the form of a program that sits sleeping on your laptop until you visit your online banking site. At that time, it wakes up and grabs your username and password with a keylogger. Others sit on your corporate network, stealing your most sensitive intellectual property.

The very strategies the Greeks used three thousand years ago to conquer the Trojans are being used today to conquer the business that *you* are in charge of running.

In turn, you must use those very same strategies—along with those utilized at various inflection points in our world history—to *protect* your businesses.

chapter one

# THIS IS WAR

*Those who cannot remember the past*
*are condemned to repeat it.*

—George Santayana (1863–1952)

W HILE IT HAS BEEN SAID BY A VARIETY OF INDIVIDUALS in a number of different ways, the maxim still holds true —if we do not know our history, we are doomed to repeat it. And if it doesn't repeat, then it certainly rhymes.

Students of history discover that many of the lessons contained therein apply to our digital lives.

Take, for example, the Peloponnesian War between Athens and Sparta. Athens was known as a highly prosperous, free-trading city-state with a great navy, while Sparta was known for its foot soldiers, discipline, and control of the surrounding regions. Pericles, who led Athens at the time, came up with five principles upon which he built a strategy to withstand the Spartan threat. These same principles can be applied in our digital lives today—particularly when it comes to business.

> *Fit to externalities.* Understand the world (i.e., the digital landscape) and its threats around you.
> *Proportionality of means and ends.* What resources do you have in terms of people, process, and technology in order to grow yet protect your organization?
> *Efficiency of leverage.* How do you leverage those resources for secondary and tertiary benefits?
> *Cohesion of internal assets.* How do you get people working together and get the highest return on investment of your

actions? This is where OKRs (Objectives and Key Results) come into play. We will analyze this in depth.

> *What can go wrong will go wrong—so be resilient when it comes to mistakes and mishaps.* You will make mistakes. They are unavoidable. Learn from them. Be anti-fragile so that you don't just return to your previous state in the wake of them. Instead, gain from the errors.

If you're familiar with the Peloponnesian War, you might already know that the Athenians eventually lost to the Spartans. Until they deviated from Periclean principles, the Athenians were winning—but deviate they did. They became more aggressive than the strategy allowed and invaded Sicily, which ended in huge losses for their army and led to their eventual defeat at the hands of Sparta. However, when they stuck to Pericles's five key components, it helped them offset the threat of a greater military power.

Adhering to a grand strategy will help you plan defenses against the asymmetric risk of an opponent who is knowledgeable and specialized in the dark arts of cybersecurity, and it will establish principles that will better serve you when the inevitability of negative events come knocking at your door.

The truth is that an organization that values its privileges more than its principles will soon lose both. Understanding the principles, values, and culture that tie into your strategy will help you defend them.

Using the lessons of history, along with the recurrent theme of "knowing thyself," will help your organization develop the right strategy, the business resilience, and the true north that will get you through both the good times and the times when things don't quite work as you'd hoped for.

## SCAR TISSUE

WE CAN LEARN from success, but the more lasting and meaningful lessons can come from failure. It's easier to learn from your own mistakes; it is harder, yet more scalable, to learn from the failure of others.

I certainly did.

Early in my career, I worked for a boutique security consulting firm that required government clearances to conduct its consulting services. I managed what was referred to as an attack and penetration team. This was a highly technical team; in fact, many of the members were referred to by their internet handles rather than their actual names. We were hired to break into networks and subsequently harden them. We were white hats (or good) hackers, tasked with finding an organization's digital security weaknesses and helping shore them up. It was then our responsibility to stand guard, essentially developing a 24/7 digital watchtower, strengthening the walls and putting guards on the tower to harden the data center.

On one particular engagement, we thought we had done a great job because our team had compromised the network, found its vulnerabilities, and exploited them. We enhanced the defenses and were in a position to defend the organization's data center.

Then I got the call. A malicious software outbreak had occurred on the very network we had secured and were now protecting.

It was a self-propagating worm known as Code Red. Code Red infected machines based on an existing vulnerability, then scanned the local network to find other machines that had that same vulnerability so it could compromise them as well. Code Red was the digital version of a zombie. Once infected, one machine infected others.

The International Standards Organization defines vulnerabilities as "a weakness of an asset or group of assets that can be exploited by one or more threats, where an asset is anything that has value to the organization, its business operations and their continuity, including information resources that support the organization's mission."

In our case, the systems were scanning so quickly and creating so much traffic on the network in the search of other machines that they created broadcast storms, where so much data was going through a fixed pipe that it eventually started to overflow. That meant we eventually started to lose connectivity to that data center, causing a *massive* outage, known today as a distributed denial of service, or DDoS, attack.

Code Red brought down the data center's availability—under my watch.

I thought I had inventoried all my assets. I thought I had inventoried all the operating systems on those assets. I thought I had inventoried all the applications on those operating systems on those assets.

I was wrong.

I had a snapshot in time of what was true—but networks are living, breathing things, and no two are the same. Every network is like a snowflake, similar but different. Not only are they different, but they're constantly changing. In mature organizations with change management oversight, someone is constantly adding some sort of new system, application, or software package. I made the mistake of thinking what we had put in place was good not just for the moment, but for the future as well.

But this oversight of mine was necessary. It developed scar tissue that contributes to my underlying philosophical view of good risk management. Also contributing to this are the lessons I've learned from some of the most important moments in the history of the world that apply directly to digital risk management.

Cyber war and overall digital risk management are analogous to the concept of a Three Block War as first described by Marine Corps General Charles Krulak in the late 1990s. This concept requires military action, peacekeeping operations, and humanitarian aid, all within three blocks. Thus, modern militaries must train to operate in all three conditions at the same time. This ties in well with the idea of having a clear, centralized vision of a strategy while enabling lower-level unit leaders to make decisions and act independently.

The three-block concept ties in well with defending a modern-day business in the digital realm. Business leaders need security teams to defend their digital domain, while also building internal cohesion through training and awareness, and, finally, tying "security by design" concepts into the earliest stages of business strategy development.

As a business professional and a leader—especially one who is not well-versed in technology but is directly involved in the management of your organization's digital security—I want you to be able to understand the importance of having an authoritative, accurate source of record of what you're defending. Further, I want you to comprehend the importance of allocating your time, effort, and resources to doing so to maximize your return on investment. In short, I want you to benefit from my scar tissue so that you can adopt some, if not all, of these philosophies for your own.

In the words of Pericles, "What you leave behind is not what is engraved in stone monuments, but what is woven into the lives of others."

## THOSE WHO WISH FOR PEACE, PREPARE FOR WAR

THE ROMANS HAD a saying:

**Si vis pacem, para bellum.**

It translates to: if you want peace, prepare for war.

If you want to have peace in the digital security space, then you need to prepare for war. I want you to see this book as a set of principles—one that allows you and your organization to navigate the digital risk of the twenty-first century by keeping your eyes on the past and your sights on the future so you can apply those lessons adroitly. In doing so, you can have better outcomes, in both business and life, by making the decision as a leader in your organization. You can invest appropriately in the new digital domain that we are increasingly dependent upon.

This book is meant to help you conceptualize highly abstract concepts through the application of analogical thinking—to increase your understanding of how you can broach more meaningful discussions about a rapidly changing space such that it improves and protects your company and your business.

What this book is *not*, however, is a how-to manual for technologists. It's not a prescriptive approach to the technological implementation of a security or privacy risk program. While cybersecurity industry leaders are referenced, this book does not belong on the shelf next to the latest and greatest hacking tome. Similarly, if you're in the weeds of an existing cybersecurity issue, then this is not the book for you.

The interpreted lessons from history within this book talk about a certain kind of discipline, and those types of disciplines can create freedom. That freedom then enables creativity, which in turn leads to meaning. Meaning leads to actualization, and actualization may culminate in enlightenment and a greater sense of purpose.

## MITRE ATT&CK® AND NIST

AS OF THE year 2020, there are approximately 350,000 malware versions identified *every day—and that number is growing.*

A new malware program is released every seven seconds. This rate has increased by 61 percent over the last year.

The cost of malware attacks is steadily rising. In 2018, companies lost 11 percent more money due to malware attacks than they did the previous year.

A website known as MITRE ATT&CK® is "a globally accessible knowledge base of adversary tactics and techniques based on real-world observations."[1] The data they've collected led to the creation of a framework that is believed to be foundational to a malicious attacker's strategy. At a high level, the framework is laid out in the following steps:

1. **Initial access**: the method an attacker uses to gain an initial connection to your business, usually through a phishing email.
2. **Execution**: the delivery of software that supports the attacker's mission.
3. **Persistence**: the establishment of connections into your business in case the initial path of entry is discovered.
4. **Privilege escalation**: the effort to become a VIP on your network.
5. **Defense evasion**: the effort to compromise your response efforts by covering their tracks.
6. **Credential access**: the access of more VIP invitations to your private network.
7. **Discovery**: the assessment and mapping of the compromised network so the attackers understand the value of the asset they now own.
8. **Lateral movement**: the movement to other assets on your network to broaden the compromise and mine and extract more value.
9. **Collection**: the process of harvesting the data elements identified, prioritized, and prepared for exfiltration.

---

[1] "ATT&CK," MITRE, accessed May 18, 2021, https://attack.mitre.org.

10. **Command and control:** the establishment of remote control of your network.

11. **Exfiltration:** the process of migrating the data identified to move it off your network.

12. **Impact:** the process of an organization coming to terms with and beginning the recovery from a breach.

You're not an attacker—but it behooves you to understand how a hacker thinks, or to at least have someone in your business playing this role. As such, while taking a deep dive into the details of each of these steps goes beyond the scope of this book, it is important to understand how detailed a plan most attackers follow to compromise your digital security.

To that end, in addition to the historical lessons from which your defense techniques can be drawn, each chapter will highlight some of the top twenty Critical Security Controls[2] (CSCs), cybersecurity best practices developed by the National Institutes of Standards and Technology[3] (NIST) and the Center for Internet Security[4] (CIS) to defend against these malicious agents and bad actors.

NIST "was founded in 1901 and is now part of the US Department of Commerce. NIST is one of the nation's oldest physical science laboratories. Congress established the agency to remove a major challenge to US industrial competitiveness at the time—a second-rate

---

[2] "CIS Controls," Center for Internet Security, accessed May 18, 2021, https://www.cisecurity.org/controls/.

[3] "About NIST," NIST, last modified June 14, 2017, https://www.nist.gov/about-nist.

[4] "About Us," Center for Internet Security, accessed May 18, 2021, https://www.cisecurity.org/about-us/.

measurement infrastructure that lagged behind the capabilities of the United Kingdom, Germany, and other economic rivals.

"From the smart electric power grid and electronic health records to atomic clocks, advanced nanomaterials, and computer chips, innumerable products and services rely in some way on technology, measurement, and standards provided by the National Institute of Standards and Technology."

In addition to the lessons from world history, these CSCs will help you have more informed questions and discussions with your security leaders on how best to invest your time, money, and effort into your digital defense profile.

To be clear, this book includes repetition of concepts such as self-actualization; validation of known knowns; and the execution and delivery of structured, discipline-balanced opportunity for creative improvisation, with a half-glass, only-the-paranoid survive perspective, embedded with the concept of continuous validation.

The power of storytelling for a domain this new is still highly abstract and challenging to manage. It cannot be emphasized enough that no matter what your experience or organizational maturity is today, the coordination and execution of sound governance are key to bringing order to this field.

With history as our guide, we are reminded that, as with military campaigns and security and privacy initiatives, there are several components or ingredients to a successful governance system. The system should include policies, standards or procedures, audit trails, organizational structures, culture, resources, and transparency. If your governing bodies are not explaining the sometimes-murky meanings of corporate initiatives laden with the latest buzzwords for greater approval, those bodies are not working.

Specifically related to security and privacy, a governance framework identifies the policies, procedures, and processes to manage and monitor the regulatory, legal, environmental, and operational requirements and ensures they are enabling the management of cybersecurity and privacy risk.

## How shall we define governance?

The World Bank defines governance as "the manner in which power is exercised in the management of a country's economic and social resources for development. Governance has been defined as the rules of the political system to solve conflicts between actors and adopt decision (legality)."

Galileo Galilei, the Tuscan physicist, mathematician, astronomer, and philosopher who contributed to the Scientific Revolution, once said, "Wine is sunlight, held together by water."

We can translate that into, "Resilience is execution, held together by governance."

Governance as a term is often over-used and misunderstood in today's business environment. This misunderstanding introduces risk into organizations, given the goal of governance is to understand how you know that you are making the right decision and have the authority to make that decision, while keeping in mind that sometimes the information you have is half wrong and half incorrect.

This true understanding allows business leaders and managers to understand the boundaries and tolerance levels within which they make decisions. While the ultimate accountability for governance resides at the board of directors or its equivalent, there are many levels to governance.

Organizations consist of multiple governing bodies at varying levels of authority. These start at the top and work their way down to operations through either formal chartered bodies or temporary groups charged with a specific focus area for a specified amount of time.

As a business grows from startup to global enterprise, it develops collections of committees, boards, and groups that are charged with governing something. There are many examples of these governing bodies, ranging from executive committees, architecture boards, risk and audit committees, steering (IT, program, project) committees, change advisory boards—the list goes on.

Each of these governing bodies sets the rules and direction for management to implement their priorities.

Now that you know what lies ahead, in the spirit of your company becoming an enlightened organization in the twenty-first century, I invite you to join me in a time machine. It's worth noting that while many of the historical examples presented in this book relate to war and battle tactics and strategies, there are equally important lessons to be derived from instances in history that occurred in times of peace.

Together we'll take a trip through the ages and pages of history to prepare for cyber war, utilizing the lessons learned from some of the most significant events in the history of our world.

Forewarned is forearmed.

chapter two

# THE CODE
# OF HAMMURABI
# AND SKIN IN
# THE GAME

*Show me the incentive, and*
*I'll show you the outcome.*

—Charlie Munger (1924–)

I N APPROXIMATELY 1771 BC, HAMMURABI, AN EMPEROR in the Babylonian Empire, decreed a set of laws to which every state in his empire had to adhere. There were 282 rules in total, and they became known as the Code of Hammurabi.

I'll spare you the tedium of exploring each of these rules, and instead focus on one.

One of the challenges Hammurabi had to reckon with was the number of architectural flaws spread throughout his empire. Architects built houses and other buildings, but those structures were so unsound in their design that the walls collapsed and killed several citizens.

Hammurabi was a student of human nature. As such, he understood the concept of "show me the incentive and I'll show you the outcome," which meant that he understood he needed to factor human incentives into the very design of his empire.

So, one of the laws he put in place was an eye-for-an-eye, a tooth-for-a-tooth type rule.

Essentially, if an architect built a structure that collapsed and resulted in someone's death, then that architect would be punished by being crushed to death by a wall.

Talk about having some skin in the game.

This rule aligned the incentives of the builders with the needs of the citizenry. Hammurabi wanted a prosperous city where both the architects and the inhabitants benefited.

It's no different in business.

In the broader sense, as a businessperson, you want a prosperous and profitable business that also considers how to manage risks and how it's protecting and safeguarding its people, assets, and interests. In fact, as a business leader, it's *critical* that you are aware of the ecological and social impact your business has on its environment.

Anecdotally, the Romans are alleged to have applied their own version of Hammurabi's Code with the Roman Law of Engineering. Once their engineers were done building a bridge, those engineers stood underneath it while the first legions marched over it. Difficult to do, I would imagine, if that bridge is over water—but you get the point. Don't just stand behind your work, stand underneath it.

But how do you align incentives such that everyone benefits?

## THE CHICKEN OR THE PIG, AND SHARED OBJECTIVES AND KEY RESULTS (OKRS)

I SOMETIMES TAKE members of my team out to a bacon-and-egg breakfast. On a team member's first breakfast, I'll ask them:

"Who's all in on this breakfast? The chicken or the pig?"

More often than not, I am met with a series of perplexed looks. Not to be deterred, I continue:

"When it comes to this breakfast plate, the chicken could lay eggs all day long, but when the heat is on, that chicken can simply walk away. But the pig? The pig is all in."

It seems funny, but it's a reminder to make long-term decisions that are meaningful and to incentivize people to be a part of those decisions.

If long-term strategic decisions are being made in your organization by temporary participants, you will not have the appropriate incentive alignment. Having strategic goals that are owned by individuals who are measured on progress toward those goals gets traction. If you are a larger organization with product, technology, and security teams, having those teams create shared OKRs on risk management goals helps achieve organizational alignment.

John Doerr is a renowned venture capitalist famous for being an early investor in Google and dozens of other companies. He introduced and evangelized for a process he learned from Andy Grove at Intel: Objectives and Key Results. OKRs are credited with being a key concept in the behemoth search engine's growth.

Doerr wrote a book on the topic called *Measure What Matters: Objectives and Key Results (OKRs): The Simple Idea that Drives 10x Growth.* In it, he points to four key values, or OKR superpowers. According to him, all good OKRs:

> **Focus** the organization on what matters
> Allow the organization to **measure progress** toward its goals
> Create **alignment** in groups
> Allow the organization to **stretch** to achieve things it wouldn't have thought possible

This powerful concept was paired with the leadership concepts espoused by legendary coach and business executive Bill Campbell in his book *Trillion Dollar Coach.*

To summarize that concept, it's teamwork that makes the dream work. The idea of removing your ego from yourself and assigning it to the business you manage helps align the orientation of company first, team second, and individual third. This is sometimes also referred to as the CEO perspective.

In philosophy, psychology, sociology, and anthropology, intersubjectivity is the sharing of subjective states by two or more individuals —shared meanings constructed by people in their interactions with each other.

Said another way, if people share a common sensibility, then they share the same definition of a situation.

This helps address organizational cognitive dissonance, which is defined by Oxford Languages as "the state of inconsistent thought, beliefs, or attitudes, especially as relating to behavioral decisions and attitude change."

Intersubjectivity is the exact opposite of solipsism, the theory that only the self is real and the self cannot be aware of anything else except itself. This means that nothing matters except you. OKRs and intersubjectivity restrain this type of toxic behavior. Imagine what would happen if your organization were to leverage this mindset, along with the power of shared OKRs, to protect your business?

Everyone would start thinking like a chief security officer.

## WHO WILL SUFFER WITH ME?

*Pain and suffering are always inevitable for
a large intelligence and a deep heart. The really great
men must, I think, have great sadness on earth.*

—Fyodor Dostoevsky (1821–1881),
*Crime and Punishment*

WHEN MAKING IMPORTANT decisions about where your company invests capital, the sort of people you hire, the sort of systems and applications you build, and how you defend them, ask yourself this question:

**Who will suffer with me when things go wrong?**

If the people who will suffer with you are in the room when you're making these big decisions, you can feel confident that you've got the right skin in the game. If the people in the room aren't going to be around when the ultimate factors of these decisions come to fruition, then you probably don't have the right stakeholders. Getting the right set of stakeholders in your organization to make important long-term decisions is key.

Consultants perfectly illustrate this concept.

On the one hand, consultants are of significant importance in helping an organization gain a more informed perspective. Consultants work in a number of different environments, which allows them to see what works and what doesn't when it comes to cybersecurity. You can certainly learn a great deal from their experience—though not all experience is the same. Just because someone has watched the *Kung Fu Panda* movies in no way means they know kung fu. Ensure the experience is rooted in the discernment that comes from learning from failure.

That said, you do not want consultants making long-term decisions for your organization. Advice on what to start, what to stop, and what to continue has value. You might want a consultant to *validate* your decisions based on what they have seen in other businesses, but their involvement should end there.

Think of consultants as tourists. They're visiting your town; they don't live there. They do their work and leave, and you're left to run the town without them. That is to say, use consultants—solicit their advice and their expertise. But when the time for impactful, long-term decisions arrives—decisions that are going to affect your company three, five, and potentially ten or more years down the road—you have to be sure that those involved in those decisions have properly aligned incentives.

You don't want anyone building your wall for you only for it to collapse on everyone after the architect has left the site.

This raises the question—or at least it should—who *are* the long-term stakeholders? Who *does* have skin in the game?

In the realm of security, privacy, and risk management, you certainly want to have your key leaders involved. A typical organization might have a chief security officer, a chief risk officer, and/or a chief privacy officer. These are the senior executives who should lead the decision-making process. They should understand the business strategy, the direction of the organization, and how they balance progress for the organization.

This balance is key. Essentially, these leaders must ask how they balance the forward momentum of the company with holistic risk management and risk tolerance.

Risk is going to occur. You can accept it, transfer it, or mitigate it, but it's something that will happen regardless. You cannot be ignorant of it. It is therefore important to have a diverse perspective on risk from employees who are both more tenured in the organization and those newer to the company. Using their experiences will create more resilient plans and strategies when it comes to those impactful, long-term decisions. But once those decisions are made, move forward practicing "division in council and unity in command."

In the realm of digital risk management, as you're considering investing in becoming more of a software-inspired organization, you have to ask yourself if you're achieving this balance.

How do you manage the risk associated with the software you're developing or the vendor relationships into which you're investing both time and money?

Do you grasp the 80/20 rule, the notion that for every dollar you invest in moving the company forward through business development, you must allocate twenty cents to your people, processes, and technologies that protect and safeguard the organization?

How are you using good governance to ensure your tradeoffs are not creating longer-term technical debt at an interest rate your organization is unable to sustain?

It is critical that you aren't simply ramping up return on equity by making investments in business advancement without investments in good underlying infrastructure and business processes to support the business growth.

If you're one of the executives holding the purse strings when it comes to the digital health of your company, that responsibility is *your* skin in the game.

## Critical Security Control (CSC) 17: Implement a Security Awareness and Training Program[5]

As you make your way through the chapters, you'll note that I refer to some of the top twenty controls more than once. I do this because there are some controls so great in importance that they cover several different scenarios.

CSC 17 is one such control. In fact, I can't say enough about just how important awareness is.

In the past, organizations had compliance training. It was one of those things that no one looked forward to completing every year. Who really wants to sit down, scroll through slides, and take a test for a certification that may or may not be immediately thrown away upon receipt?

At the same time, there were—and still are—employee engagement surveys that reach out to team members to ask how happy they are at work. What could the company be doing better?

Both examples are representative of a legacy approach to awareness and training—but today, organizations are including more and more awareness training for their employees. Reactions to answers on surveys are more bespoke, reminding higher-ups to take certain actions based on those responses.

Cybersecurity is going in a similar direction, putting awareness at the forefront, and the tone of this awareness starts at the top.

CEOs have to talk about the fact that cybersecurity is everyone's job. Some organizations will have a dedicated chief security officer

---

[5] "Implement a Security Awareness and Training Program," Center for Internet Security, accessed May 18, 2021, https://www.cisecurity.org/controls/implement-a-security-awareness-and-training -program/.

(CSO), while others might not—but if the culture is such that security, awareness, and risk management belong to everyone in the company, then you have alignment.

Solutions exist today that evolved from traditional corporate compliance security training. They factor in the behavior of the employees. For example, if someone didn't pay attention in their training and clicked on a phishing attack as a result, they would be elected to have more training regarding awareness about those types of attacks. Hammurabi understood this when he composed the Code in Babylon. It was essentially a code of conduct.

Organizations need to understand what's working and what's not, take best practices for security and awareness, and implement more bespoke training. This prevents the idea of "set it and forget it" attitudes, and the culture becomes one of ongoing communication with the employee base. Provide quarterly updates about the latest threats. Utilize a monthly newsletter that integrates fun quizzes to test or refresh employees' knowledge. Incentivize people to listen and learn.

Consider the science of reinforcement. How do you periodically continue to reinforce key ideas so that your employees become better versions of themselves? This idea ties closely, in many ways, to good marketing. When any big brand wants you to purchase their product, you see it everywhere—in the news, on the internet, in the daily paper. There could be numerous different touchpoints for a successful campaign. Training and awareness are no different. You want to touch your employees regarding risk awareness through multiple different vehicles.

The enlightened organization of the future is a risk-aware organization. If you want to take a course designed for executives to learn more about cybersecurity management, I recommend

Stanford's Advanced Cybersecurity Certificate Program run by author, entrepreneur, and PhD Neil Daswani. Neil is the author of the book *Big Breaches: Cybersecurity Lessons for Everyone*. His article "The Seven Habits of Highly Effective Security" is a great way to understand risk management behaviors built to last.

## THE AIRBAG VERSUS THE SWORD

SO HOW DO you align incentives to make the best long-term decisions?

For an unconventional perspective on incentives and risk, try Nassim Taleb's one-week seminars in New York held at the Princeton Club, where he brings together an eclectic group of people—financial experts, survivalists, military personnel, and mathematicians. The seminar is a seven-day treat with fun topics for risk practitioners.

I learned of a discussion generated there, and it caught my attention.

A group of mathematicians from Stony Brook University was talking about incentives in the context of the fact that roughly sixty-five thousand people die in car accidents every year. Their argument was that one of the reasons for this number was that drivers' incentives were misaligned.

We all know that if you get into a head-on collision, an airbag will deploy, and you may be protected. Their argument was that the airbag provides the wrong incentive. The mathematicians theorized that to truly reduce vehicular mortalities, airbags should be replaced with a sword.

Think about it. How much more cautiously would people drive if they knew that a head-on collision would result in a sword to the face?

It seems ridiculous on its surface, but for a group of people who look at the world through numbers and statistical probabilities, the argument makes a great deal of sense. It certainly caught my attention—and the concept stuck with me. It made me consider the question:

**How do we create the right incentive model for organizations to enhance their cybersecurity efforts?**

Tying performance to compensation is certainly one way to go. Most companies have some form of annual performance review, one that is typically made up of specific, measurable, achievable, relevant, and time-bound (SMART) goals. Those goals should then tie into departmental milestones, and those milestones should tie into the organizational strategy. If you align your incentive compensation program with those business outcomes, you can help people and teams make better decisions because they know that if they don't, it will actually lighten their pockets. That's skin in the game.

Want to find digital zombies on your network? Then reward the hunters. Many organizations refer to this as a bug bounty program. If someone identifies a software bug, they receive a financial reward. There are companies that specialize in this tactic. You can hire an organization of hackers who will attempt to find problems in your security defenses, and if they do, they're rewarded with a bonus.

You don't have to go to the outside, however, and you're not just looking for software-based bugs—processes can have them too. Incentivize employees to find a process flaw and call it out—but not in a way that casts blame. These discoveries are highlighted as an area of improvement. The callout is reviewed by a group of the employee's peers, and if they've actually discovered a meaningful issue that can be corrected, they receive a trophy and a cash reward.

When looking to achieve this alignment of incentives, it is critical that you do not create a fear-based environment. Life is too short to live in a state of fear. We want to lean in toward positive growth outcomes by incentivizing people with recognition and rewards for doing the right thing rather than punishing them for the wrong thing. It's the classic carrot and the stick. Start with the carrot—don't use the stick until absolutely necessary.

## INCENTIVES IN ACTION

LO AND BEHOLD, by aligning incentives with (rather horrible) outcomes, the building structures within Babylon improved.

A thousand years later, the Babylonian Empire continued to build on the Code of Hammurabi principles, which resulted in and contributed to one of the seven wonders of the ancient world, the Hanging Gardens of Babylon, built roughly between 605 and 562 BC—beautiful gardens built on the walls of a now structurally sound empire.

You can trace this great empire, its architectural accomplishments, and the ultimate beauty of the hanging gardens back to Hammurabi's fundamental understanding of human nature and how he tied it to his underlying foundational code to build that empire.

While Hammurabi's Code was far more stick than carrot, the lesson here is clear. In creating our cybersecurity principles, we must ensure that those involved in that creation are long-term stakeholders who stand to lose as much as they do to gain. This notion is foundational to the other elements that will build a digital security framework that can be agile, flexible, and built to last.

chapter three

# THE SPARTAN THREE HUNDRED AND MANAGING THE ATTACK SURFACE

*...With enough leverage, a finger could overturn the world.*

—Jean-Jacques Rousseau (1712–1778)

D O YOU REMEMBER THE FIRST STORY YOUR PARENTS told you?

I do.

The first story I learned as a child was about a Spartan boy.

The child had been running in the field when he came upon a baby fox, which he captured with his bare hands. He hid the fox under his cloak to bring it back to his barracks at the Spartan agoge, or training center. Once Spartan boys reached the age of seven, they began their training to become warriors. When he arrived, he and the other boys in training were called to attention by their trainers. The boy stood at attention but kept the fox hidden under his cloak.

But the fox was hungry. While hidden under the cloak, it began gnawing at the boy's stomach.

At that moment, the boy had a choice. He could stand down from attention to let the fox go, losing his discipline but saving him from being bitten—or he could hold onto the fox, maintaining his self-control and self-discipline.

As the story goes, the boy did not stand down. He held onto the fox as it chewed away at his stomach. He did not flinch. He did not falter. When he was finally released from attention, he ran back to his barracks in the agoge, where he lay down and eventually died from his wound.

The story of the boy and the fox is an admittedly morbid one, and perhaps that's why it stuck with me. But it also served to spark a fascination in me with ancient Greece, and Sparta in particular.

In this chapter, we'll focus on the Spartans themselves—in particular, the famous three hundred. The discipline instilled in Spartan warriors from a very early age helped them to save the Western world —depending upon your perspective—from the invasion of the Persian Empire. The methods they used to do so apply quite well to today's cybersecurity concerns.

The Persians had assembled the largest army the world had ever seen. Some scholars have suggested that it was made up of over one million men. In 480 BC, this was an unimaginable number given there were only an estimated one hundred million people living at that time.

Think about that.

One out of every one hundred living human beings on the planet at that time was in this Persian army. Now, extrapolate that using today's numbers. Nearly eight billion people are presently populating the earth. In current terms, that would mean an army of eighty million soldiers. For context, in 2020, China has the world's largest standing army with an estimated 2.1 million soldiers.

This is to say the Persian numbers were staggering. (It should be noted that other scholars estimate that the Persian Army may have consisted of closer to 150,000 soldiers, but even that number was quite large given the population estimates. Whichever number is correct, the fact remains that the Persians managed to assemble the largest army ever seen with the design of conquering the Greek city-states.)

The trouble was that the Greeks within the city-states weren't necessarily getting along very well, and at the time of the invasion, the Spartans were celebrating one of their holidays. They were at odds with each other about whether or not they should break off from the traditions of the holiday and meet the Persians in battle.

Sparta had a two-king approach. While one king remained in the city to honor the holiday, the other, King Leonidas, decided to take three hundred Spartan soldiers to engage with the Persians at a place called Thermopylae, also known as The Hot Gates. He chose to meet them there because as the Persians disembarked from their ships, they had to march through the narrow strait that was Thermopylae. It was a logical place for the Spartans to make their stand.

History tells us that the Spartan's number was complemented by approximately seven hundred Thespians, nine hundred Helots, and four hundred Devens, but the Spartans' three hundred soldiers made up the bulk of the professional warriors. In terms of strict volume, the Greeks were vastly outnumbered—as a reported one million men faced off against thousands of Greeks, with only three hundred highly trained combatants.

The Spartan Army held the Persians off for three days, enough time for the Greek city-states to understand the threat and for them to mobilize and develop a strategy of their own to fight against the Persians.

In those three days, the Spartan three hundred valiantly defended against the onslaught of the Persians, though they all eventually died a noble death, much like the boy and the fox. They lost their lives in defense of their home and bought time for the city-states to rally and eventually defeat the Persians.

But how? How did an army a fraction of the size of the Persian dreadnought manage this incredible feat? It wasn't only because they were highly disciplined, trained, and motivated soldiers.

It's also because they managed the attack surface.

## FUNNEL THE ATTACK

IN ADDITION TO bringing their skill and focus to battle, the Spartans managed where they would defend against the Persian attack by funneling their opponents into a narrow stretch of land. That way, only a concentrated number of their massive force could attack the Spartans and their allies at any given time. Not only that, but this placement also ensured that the Spartans could only be attacked from the front—they could not be encircled by the Persian forces.

This same concept—this idea of managing the attack surface—is a key fundamental principle in defending an organization when it comes to cybersecurity and digital risk management.

A one-year-old company with a tight technology inventory of systems and applications it owns is infinitely easier to defend than one with a broad attack surface. As that company grows its very success can create a weak underbelly that will eventually put it at greater risk. It must build more and more servers, applications, and endpoints—and each of those needs to be defended. It follows that the more technology the company has, the more that technology needs to be defended—and this could mean hundreds of thousands of servers, hundreds of thousands of laptops, and desktops. This opens that organization up to various attack vectors.

If you can narrow your attack surface—if you can reduce the number of servers that you need to defend, or at least channel them through a choke point as the Spartans did at Thermopylae—it can translate into much better outcomes for your company.

For example, if you architect a network topology that is flat, then everything can talk to everything. That is a massively wide attack surface and incredibly difficult to defend. But if you architect zones, you are instilling security by design on an architectural level. Creating zones means that only portions of your topology can talk to other portions. This is accomplished through a centralized choke point that serves as the only point of access for connecting to other zones in the network.

Your business's network has user credentials, commonly referred to as user accounts. They also have privileged accounts that belong to administrators who have the rights to move about the network to perform various duties, sometimes referred to as domain or enterprise admins. These accounts have God Right—they can perform virtually any action in the digital domain. If they are allowed to connect to any system and any application across your organization's network topology, then it becomes quite challenging to maintain attribution, traceability, and containment.

However, if you design an architecture where those privileged accounts first have to go to the aforementioned choke point, then you have narrowed the scope of attack. Now, when a malicious attack or hacker assaults your network, they will first have to focus on the choke point—the digital Thermopylae that you've created—to even begin to access your network.

Best of all, that choke point is *far* easier to maintain, monitor, and protect than all of your cloud or on-premises assets. The combination of privileged account management, heightened access controls, locking down the assets from which privileged activity may occur, and enhanced monitoring of the activity on those accounts enables a more manageable environment.

## Critical Security Controls 4 and 9: Controlled Use of Administrative Privileges[6] and Limitation and Control of Network Ports, Protocols, and Services[7]

There is a concept called the sliding scale of security where you have your highest return on investment through architecture, first and foremost. The Systems Administration Network Security (SANS) group published a white paper on the topic specifically addressing that how you use your architecture to structure your digital landscape has a significant effect on how you defend it.

As cited on *www.sans.org*,[8] "The SANS Institute was established in 1989 as a cooperative research and education organization. Its programs now reach more than 165,000 security professionals around the world. A range of individuals from auditors and network administrators to chief information security officers are sharing the lessons they learn and are jointly finding solutions to the challenges

---

[6] "CIS Control 4: Controlled Use of Administrative Privileges," Center for Internet Security, accessed May 18, 2021, https://www.cisecurity.org/controls/controlled-use-of-administrative-privileges/.

[7] "CIS Control 9: Limitation and Control of Network Ports, Protocols and Services." Center for Internet Security, accessed May 18, 2021, https://www.cisecurity.org/controls/limitation-and -control-of-network-ports-protocols-and-services/.

[8] "About SANS Institute," SANS, accessed May 18, 2021, https://www.sans.org/about/.

they face. At the heart of SANS are the many security practitioners in varied global organizations from corporations to universities working together to help the entire information security community.

"SANS is a respected source for information security training and security certification in the world. It also develops, maintains, and makes available at no cost the largest collection of research documents about various aspects of information security, and it operates the internet's early warning system—the Internet Storm Center."

Administrative privilege is of the utmost importance. There are the typical users on your network, there are the privileged users, and then there are your domain administrators, people who have above-and-beyond privileged access across your network.

Those privileges must be treated like the key to the kingdom. You need to control them. You need to limit the number of users that have that precious access. Those who have it must be required to have a higher degree of authentication through multifactor authentication. You must require them to use dedicated endpoints that are not surfing the internet and/or receiving email. Additionally, these special users should use choke points to log in and conduct their administrative activities across the network.

Essentially, you must tighten the areas of control, thereby narrowing the attack surface such that when an attacker is seeking those privileged accounts, they find less of them. This limits the places an attacker can go after the various assets on your network. If you do end up compromised, you go directly to your choke point because you know it is the island that has been attacked and from which all other subsequent attacks originate. You funnel where the bad actors can go.

In the case of your network ports, protocols, and services, recognize that when you open a system or application, all of the network ports are open in most cases. You need to carefully disable anything that will not be in explicit use as it again reduces the number of pathways an attacker can use to navigate your internal network. You create a centralized choke point, thereby managing your attack surface and leveraging your digital defense capabilities.

A larger opponent, such as a group of hackers or an opposing nation, will want to take advantage of their breadth and depth of strength—to be an asymmetric adversary. They want to leverage the fact that they only have to be right once, where you have to be right each and every time. They want a broad area, a wide field of battle where, at the worst, they can "spray and pray" when they launch their attacks, in the hopes that they can compromise some of your data.

When you force their efforts into a narrow gate, you make attackers thread the eye of the needle. You force them through a choke point you control. That's a desirable position for you to be in.

## DON'T BE POUND FOOLISH

AS AN EXECUTIVE who doesn't have the technical know-how but is empowered to create the budget for your technology teams, it's important to know that the creation of this digital Thermopylae requires an investment in your architectural design. While more is said on budget later in the book, please keep in the back of your mind that budgeting is an input, while sound risk management is an outcome. The two may not always correlate.

There's also an investment to be made in understanding your network topology.

How is it zoned? Are segments created on the network? How do your accounts, particularly your privileged ones, navigate those various segments? How are the privileged access management accounts maintained?

This can be managed through architectural design and network and application reconfiguration. And the truth is, this is a thinking and planning effort. You need to know where you are, where you're going, and how you want to go about designing and reconfiguring.

Investment isn't just about dollars and cents. Investing means the intellectual rigor of owning your past decisions, acknowledging your present state, and envisioning and executing on the delivery of a digital future. This digital future begins with architecture, which lays the foundation for more effective defense measures built on the solid foundation of a well-thought-out plan.

Effectively illustrated by SANS, the sliding scale of security shows that the highest return on investment (ROI) in terms of value toward security comes from architecture.

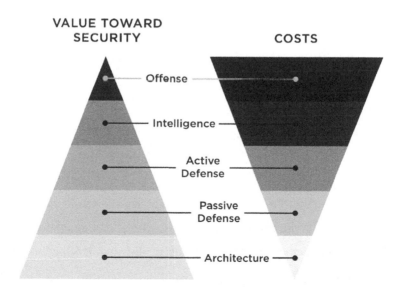

**ARCHITECTURE**
The planning, establishing, and upkeep of systems with security in mind

**PASSIVE DEFENSE**
Systems added to the architecture to provide reliable defense or insight against threats without consistent human interaction

**ACTIVE DEFENSE**
The process of analysts monitoring for, responding to, and learning from adversaries internal to the network

**INTELLIGENCE**
Collecting data, exploiting it into information, and producing intelligence

**OFFENSE**
Legal countermeasures and self-defense actions against an adversary

## YOU CAN'T SET IT AND FORGET IT

CYBERSECURITY AND DIGITAL risk management are a journey, not a destination.

One of the fundamental principles is that the efficacy of controls degrades over time. This principle is one referenced by one of the security industry's thought leaders, Phil Venables, former Chief Information Risk Officer at Goldman Sachs. His blog, www.philvenables. com, is a bookmarked site I visit regularly. There he talks about what is variable and what is invariable of security risk management. The degradation of efficacy, or as Phil labels it, "Entropy is King," will ring true forever.

Risk exceptions/acceptances to those controls accelerate ossification. They make your controls more brittle and likely to break. New systems and applications are added and removed. Access for users is granted and removed. Employees move around within the company. Other employees leave and their identities, role-based access control, and privileges must be managed.

All of this must be monitored and maintained. You cannot set it and forget it. That is the exact opposite of good, holistic digital risk management.

Your team might create the perfect network architecture today. You might even get it certified by a third party, for example, and they'll tell you that it is secure.

Today.

But guess what? The changes on the network that will happen this evening and tomorrow will change that posture and may introduce risks that you might not have considered before. This is why the discipline of continuous validation is so essential as you trust but verify. In fact, flip that around—verify, then trust.

Recall that King Leonidas and his Spartans were able to defend their attack surface for three days and nights—but they were eventually undone. A separate path, unbeknownst to them, was shared with the Persians by an insider with a grudge against the Spartans. This path allowed the Persians to circle up behind the Spartans and eventually defeat them. The Spartans didn't know that there was a weakness, a vulnerability in their attack surface. They didn't know their flank could be exposed. It's the equivalent of an undetected critical security vulnerability being shared by an insider of your business to an outside attacker.

The lesson here applies to your digital security. Just because you think you know where your choke points are once you've established them doesn't mean you should get comfortable. In fact, you should be constantly hunting for threats on your network, whether they be from digital intruders, an insider threat, or architectural gotchas—changes that occur that expose your digital flank and can be leveraged by an attacker. We all have digital zombies roaming our networks, and they can bite when we least expect it. We will always have vulnerabilities on our networks. Software companies identify and publish vulnerabilities daily, monthly, and quarterly. A recent study suggests[9] 96 percent of all business applications produce vulnerabilities that require either a patch or configuration fix. Organizations rely on compensating controls in place with layers of defense to take the gross risk of a vulnerability to a lower net risk.

The larger you are as an organization, the more critically important this becomes—particularly if you're a company in the practice of buying other companies.

Case in point: Company X.

## COMPANY X

WE WON'T USE the name of companies that have suffered large data breaches in the past (see Neil Daswani's well-researched book for specifics), but chances are better than good that you know the story of

---

[9] "New Contrast Security Report Finds 96% of Business Applications Contain Vulnerabilities as Attack Volume Grows 60%," *Intrado GlobeNewswire*, July 24, 2020, https://www.globenewswire.com/news-release/2020/07/24/2067350/0/en/New-Contrast-Security-Report-Finds-96-of-Business-Applications-Contain-Vulnerabilities-as-Attack-Volume-Grows-60.html.

the Company X breach. It had the potential to be an existential event for the company. The attack exposed millions of records and cost the company hundreds of millions, if not billions, of dollars. A class-action lawsuit against it is still pending as I write this book.

Company X was the perfect example of a business that was a victim of its own success. They were growing internationally and acquiring new companies. However, network integrations from new companies can be exceedingly difficult. Company X may have invested in a robust network, but if a company they bought didn't have the same level of technology hygiene, all of that potential risk was assumed into Company X's own environment. This is one of the many challenges of mergers and acquisitions.

Based on its growth and acquisition strategy, the company had numerous different technologies to manage—and that technology was eventually exploited through a web server that had default credentials enabled on it. This meant that it was possible for an attacker to log in with these well-known credentials and weave their way through the Company X environment, exploit some of their software vulnerabilities, and compromise a dataset that affected millions of individuals. Many executives, including the CEO, had to resign as a result of this breach.

Company X is the perfect example of a broad attack surface where those responsible may not have even known the aspects of their own network based on a mergers and acquisition strategy.

The Spartans managed their entry and exfiltration points, just as you should do with your digital landscape. You must control those points as well as be aware of exactly how much data can enter and leave your organization. If you don't have the correct retention policies in place with teeth and traction, you'll find yourself holding data that not only yields no economic benefit but may pose risks from a breach perspective.

# chapter four

# MARCUS AURELIUS, SUN TZU, AND THE ART OF DIGITAL WAR

*If you know the enemy and
know yourself, you need not fear the
result of a hundred battles.*

—Sun Tzu (544–496 BC)

A S YOU MAY KNOW, MARCUS AURELIUS WAS A ROMAN emperor. What you might not know is that he was not the son of nobility—he was adopted by Emperor Casey.

Casey saw in Aurelius qualities that he believed would make Marcus a great leader, and so Marcus (and his brother, Lucius Aurelius Verus) became the co-caesars of Rome—but they went about their lives in two very different ways.

Lucius Verus was a decadent individual, focused on bacchanalian self-indulgence, what the Greeks called *hedonia,* or a hedonistic life focused on pleasure. Marcus was more of a thoughtful introvert, who practiced *eudaimonia*, or a life focused on virtue. In moments of solitude, Marcus began learning what we now refer to as Stoic philosophy, which was started by a Phoenician merchant named Zeno.

Zeno was a successful merchant who traveled the Mediterranean transporting fermented oysters. Interestingly, these fermented oysters produced a needle point of purple ink. That minute amount of ink was extracted from oysters to color royal garments. The uncommon color indicated the rarity and cost of the garment; it took tens of thousands of oysters to color a single garment. This ancient tradition has been passed down through the centuries and, as such, royal ceremonial garments are often purple. In fact, Queen Elizabeth I once forbade the use of this color throughout England to preserve the sanctity of its symbolism.

One day, Zeno was shipwrecked in Greece. While stranded there, he began to ponder his own life and took up learning about the different schools of philosophy of the period. He took elements of what he learned and developed his own school of thought, which became known as Stoicism. Stoicism, as Zeno developed it, was about cultivating a sense of self-control and grit, wherein an individual would not catastrophize the things going on in the world around them—in fact, they would bring a sense of equanimity and understanding to it.

It was this philosophy that Marcus became interested in as a young boy. He was particularly intrigued by the teachings of the philosopher Junius Rusticus (AD 100–170), who also mentored Marcus. During this mentorship, Marcus kept a journal about his views of the world around him. Time went on, Lucius passed away, and Marcus became the sole emperor of Rome. Marcus continued with his journal entries throughout his reign, and they became known as the *Meditations*.

He had no intention of publishing them. He was not writing a philosophical perspective. Marcus was simply noting his own view of the world. Former president Bill Clinton cites *Meditations* as his favorite book of all time, and former secretary of defense James Mattis states that he carries it with him in all his travels. (I personally keep a copy on the nightstand by my bed.)

Some of the core, foundational concepts in *Meditations* revolve around the idea of knowing oneself.

Who are you? What is important to you? What does it mean to live a virtuous life?

This concept introduced a holistic perspective of life and insight, such as what is not good for the hive cannot be good for the bee—the idea that every one of us is part of a broader holistic ecosystem.

# KNOW YOUR DIGITAL SPACE— THEN KEEP LOOKING

JUST AS ONE must know oneself, a company must know its digital realm.

*All* of it.

We've discussed how to manage your attack surface, but you can't get to that point unless you foundationally know the environment in which you exist today and all of the assets (endpoints, software, etc.) that are a part of it.

Organizations need to have a foundational discipline in technology asset management. That umbrella should expand to cover not just the servers on your network or the desktops and laptops you host, but also the cloud-based technologies that you subscribe to through software as a service (SaaS) or infrastructure as a service (IaaS), wherein you're leveraging someone else's infrastructure. This also includes the vendors you depend on and supply-chain risk management.

This has now expanded to what is known as the internet of things (IoT) devices. The internet-enabled television, fridge, or toaster all have internet protocol (IP) addresses assigned to them. Each one of these endpoints can be attacked and exploited, in most cases simply to generate traffic in mass against another IP address as part of DDoS attacks.

We must know about and guard each of these areas. That requires a discipline of continuous learning, continuous monitoring and validation, and continuous improvement.

Know those assets. Know those systems, those applications, the cloud-based services, the vendors you depend on, and the supply chain that your vendors depend on to provide business value to your clients. This concept harkens back to Marcus's insights about being part of a broader ecosystem and how we all are impacted by the world around us. Understanding all of this allows for a more bespoke approach to protecting your organization's value at risk (VaR).

VaR is a popular method for financial risk measurement because it calculates the probability of an investment generating a loss during a given time period and against a given level of confidence. It can be calculated for either one asset, a portfolio of multiple assets, or an entire company. Knowing how all of your assets work together supports greater clarity on VaR; more precise VaR calculations complement a holistic risk management approach to defending yourself in the digital age.

The Ponemon Institute conducts studies on topics that support thought leadership and marketing objectives. The institute is best known for its annual *Cost of a Data Breach Report,* which is sponsored by IBM, and the annual *Global Encryption Trends Study*, sponsored by Entrust. The institute is a great source for understanding the cost of a breach and has influenced how the industry measures the cost of VaR being breached.

The institute provides industry estimates on the value of a lost credit card or an individual's personally identifiable information (PII). Most recently, this value has been estimated at approximately $200 per record. This means when a company loses its client's PII, the loss due to the investigations, associated credit monitoring, reputational damage, and potential regulatory penalty averages out to $200 per record. So, if a company were to experience a breach of one million PII records, it would result in an estimated VaR of approximately $200 million.

In other words—know thyself, know thy apps, know thy data, and know thy digital identities.

> ### Critical Security Controls 1, 2, and 16:
> ### Inventory and Control of Hardware Assets,[10]
> ### Inventory and Control of Software Assets,[11] and
> ### Account Monitoring and Control[12]
>
> The fundamental concept of knowing thyself translates directly into the first two critical security controls.
>
> One of the things organizations commonly struggle with are the existential questions: Who am I? What am I? What do I have?
>
> What makes up my technology stack? What are the IP addresses that represent my brand? What systems and applications, laptops, desktops, and IoT (internet of things) endpoints compromise the ecosystem that I must defend?
>
> It's for this reason that NIST called out the first CSC as inventory and control of hardware assets because organizations, big and small, have hardware that connects to the internet—and the list of equipment that does so is continuing to grow. The more those organizations connect new devices to their network, the more items they have to worry about.

---

[10] "CIS Control 1: Inventory and Control of Hardware," Center for Internet Safety, accessed May 18, 2021, https://www.cisecurity.org/controls/inventory-and-control-of-hardware-assets/.

[11] "CIS Control 2: Inventory and Control of Software," Center for Internet Safety, accessed May 18, 2021, https://www.cisecurity.org/controls/inventory-and-control-of-software-assets/.

[12] "CIS Control 16: Account Monitoring and Control," Center for Internet Safety, accessed May 18, 2021, https://www.cisecurity.org/controls/account-monitoring-and-control/.

Just as challenging is the software component (CSC 2). The inventory and control of hardware assets is a little more black-and-white—but what about the software both you *and* your clients rely on?

In a world where everyone is accelerating their digital transformation to be cloud-first or even cloud-native (meaning the services that you offer are based in someone else's data center), you still need to understand the risk associated with doing so. Additionally, with these changes enterprises rapidly expand their digital formation efforts, and they may be unwittingly increasing their risks or attack surface.

NIST made these CSCs a priority because inventorying and controlling software is quite difficult to do—but it's well worth the discipline and execution because once you know yourself (your systems, applications, and their associated vulnerabilities), you can apply the proper defense architecture.

When you implicitly don't trust any device (the zero-trust model) and commit yourself to the true knowledge of your assets, you can make insightful decisions about the construction and management of your digital defense.

Account monitoring and control (CSC 16) is not just about systems and applications, but also your user IDs. Perhaps some IDs haven't been used in some time and are now sitting dormant. These are the digital equivalent of zombies, whether they're virtual machines that have been stood up and uncared for or user accounts that have gone dormant because an employee left, and that account wasn't deleted. Because they haven't been deactivated, they risk compromise.

# SUN TZU AND MODERN CYBER WAR

SUN TZU (544–496 BC) was the author of *The Art of War*. He was a Chinese general, military strategist, writer, and philosopher. Although Sun Tzu is generally credited as the author of *The Art of War*, there is evidence that he began writing it and other military strategists continued to contribute to it over a hundred-year time period, finally resulting in the version of the book we know today. Regardless, it has gone on to be considered one of the greatest books on strategy ever written.

Sun Tzu asked the question: how does one fight a battle?

Much of his answer is applicable to today's digital world.

Sun Tzu stated that if you know thyself *and* know thy enemy, you will win a hundred battles. This extends beyond the foundational concepts of just knowing yourself, your environment, and your systems applications. You also have to know your enemy, which is tricky to do in this realm because attribution is so difficult. The work-around here is to understand and know your threat profile.

If you're a pharmaceutical company making a next-generation cancer drug, you have a very different threat profile than a financial institution that processes credit cards. A conglomerate, international business advisory or a nation-state that is investing in the pharmaceutical space might want to target you if you've got a promising next-generation cancer drug. If you're a financial institution, you're much more likely to be attacked by a digital fraudster who is looking to quickly use stolen information or resell it on the black market known as the dark web.

It's critical to understand your organizational threat profile and your VaR. Your intellectual property will help you tune your digital defenses so that they're not just leveraging your own internal environment but are also bespoke to the threat environment you are in.

You might even be facing internal threats.

A sophisticated attacker won't just target the asset—they'll target the human being associated with the target, whether a custodian or a link in the supply chain. If you're dealing with a sophisticated adversary, they will socially engineer your employees. They might fish an employee, send them an email, get them to click on a link, and gain access to your system. They might try to blackmail an employee by sending them a message that says, for example, they are in possession of a compromising photo of said employee. They can leverage this photo (imagined or not) by telling the employee to either stand down during an attack launch or to help them stage the attack from within.

Worse yet, they might implant a contractor or full-time employee within your organization.

Let's say an attacker is targeting a large chemical corporation. The first phase of the attack will utilize traditional cyberattacks through phishing emails, luring employees to compromised sites that host malicious software, or any other number of techniques.

Should those efforts prove fruitless, the attacker then sends in contractors to the target company to get internal access to its network.

If that doesn't work, the next step is arranging for employees working with the attacker to be hired on to the target company. If all else fails, large players with black box budgets will invest in the target chemical corporation to obtain the intellectual property they're after.

The FBI is constantly looking for these types of internal threats. I sat next to a technology executive from a prestigious university and asked what their biggest worry was. I assumed it would have something to do with technology implementation. Instead, they told me they worried about foreign governments planting students with government-certified credentials in their school. Of course, these were not actual students but spies walking the corridors of the university and harvesting intellectual property that's being codeveloped by the university along with the companies they work with.

In the realm of digital defense, it's guerilla warfare 24/7, which is why you need to tune your defenses to understand the threat profile you're facing.

The unfortunate truth is the more we connect to things, the more things we have to worry about being compromised. There was a time when digital security teams only had to worry about the server, laptop or desktop, and applications. That was the common attack surface that we needed to defend.

As we're adopting more internet-of-things devices, the compromise of these devices will begin to lead to the internal compromise of organizations. While this hasn't really surfaced as of yet, it's going to happen.

In recent years, an attacker compromised a larger number of IoT from televisions to DVRs to toasters—we're talking millions of these devices. The attackers then had all of these devices point to a DNS provider, which created an unbelievable amount of traffic in the form of TCP packets to bring down that service. It was known as the 2016 Dyn DDoS attack, and it brought the company to its knees because they were unable to service their clients. It was a perfect example of leveraging the IoT and a broader attack surface to weaponize it against another company.

This company was a victim of the industry simply not having yet acknowledged the possible threat posed by the IoT. They were the victims of poor technology, poor hygiene management, and an industry that is getting ahead of itself. These devices are rolling out without good security to accompany them.

The technology that empowers us also imperils us. In the spirit of Sun Tzu, we must know our enemy and understand our digital risk profile with great clarity.

Organizations must consider how they are adopting IoT and ask questions such as:

> Are we inventorying what we put on our network?
> Do we know *exactly* what it is and what it does?
> How do we maintain and configure it?
> How do we patch it?

Considering these questions builds the foundation of not just knowing thyself but knowing thy enemy.

## YOUR DIGITAL "FINANCIAL STATEMENT"

AS AN ORGANIZATIONAL executive, how do you apply the analogical thinking of "know thyself" to help you think through the digital domain?

To answer that, let's consider how a financial executive, for example, thinks about the financial statements of a publicly traded organization. A resource for them might be Sarbanes-Oxley, which helps organizations trust the financials that they publish via a strict set of controls. SOX requires an internal control report that states management is responsible for an adequate internal control structure for its financial records. SOX requires formal data security policies, communication of data security policies, and consistent enforcement of data security policies and controls enforcing:

> Separation of duties
> Access control
> Required approvals
> Asset audits
> Reconciliation
> Data backups

Executives need validation around different components that result in the numbers that they publish to the market about the health and well-being of their financial "house." Typically, organizations will have a chief financial officer (CFO) or a chief accounting officer (CAO) who contributes to the creation of this publication.

These officers need to work throughout the corridor to gather sources of information from employees across the company that they know and trust. Eventually, the CEO and CFO sign off on those financials, and when they are published, the markets will base some of their activity on those financial results.

That mindset should be applied to how you think about your technology assets. The financial executive has a discipline and demand for knowing where their numbers come from. How did a department arrive at this number? Who has access to it?

When it comes to your digital assets you have to have the same discipline and demand for knowledge. Do you know all the assets on your network? What process do you have in place to inventory those systems, applications, and vendor relationships? How often are they validated? Who is scrutinizing all of this, outside of the owner, so that there is some level of independence in your process? How does it all roll up into a risk appetite for an organization?

The mindset, discipline, and methodologies that organizations and executives use today in creating their financial statements can be applied in creating your digital financial statement—or your digital risk statement—as part of a greater organizational risk appetite statement (RAS). This RAS itself is the total amount of risk your organization is prepared to accept. It is compromised by a series of individual risk tolerance measures and their associated thresholds to better understand the state of your environment.

Knowing thyself and knowing thy enemy aren't just pithy catchphrases when it comes to digital security. They are foundational principles to maintaining the hygiene of your company's digital domain.

Marcus Aurelius once said:

> "Never let the future disturb you. You will meet it, if you have to, with the same weapons of reason which today arm you against the present."

Armed with knowing thyself as a foundational principle, you will be better equipped to defend your present while remaining at the ready for a future cyber war.

chapter five

# RED SWANS
# AND THE KNOWN
# KNOWNS THAT
# JUST AIN'T SO

*Only the paranoid survive.*

—Andrew Grove (1936–2016),
Intel CEO

D URING THE 2008–2009 FINANCIAL CRISIS, AUTHOR NASIM Taleb published *The Black Swan*. The book's central theme was that probability analysis can't be applied to all aspects of risk in life. There are times when you're going to encounter black swans, the unknown unknowns that pop up, much like the coronavirus pandemic that occurred as I was writing this book.

For the longest time, the Western world thought white swans were the only type of swans in existence. Then, with the colonization of Australia by the British in the late 1600s, the black swan was discovered. It was a shock to biologists; they had discovered an unknown unknown.

There was some editorial commentary that Taleb was fortunate with his timing of the book, saying that even a broken clock is right twice a day. Either way, when the book was released, it garnered a lot of attention and made readers think about risk through Taleb's perspective of different types of swans. The white swans represent the known knowns. Gray swans represent the known unknowns, and the black swans are the unknown unknowns.

When it comes to cybersecurity, there are things we worry about —the known threats of DDoS attacks, malicious attacks from nation-states, and cybercriminal gangs. Then there are the known unknowns. Who is the attacker working from the inside of your company? Who's trading data illegally? How do you continue looking for those kinds of threats and setting up the proper monitoring for them?

In the digital realm, black swans are the threats you can't really prepare for because you don't know what they are or will be. That attack might turn out to be a brand-new self-propagating computer virus or a worm that the world hasn't seen before and for which there is no antidote or antivirus solution. While you can't know what these attacks will be ahead of time, you *can* introduce processes that allow you to emerge from them stronger.

The coronavirus pandemic beautifully demonstrates how we can emerge from black swans better. The pandemic required every industry that was capable of doing so to shift to a work-from-home model. Companies that had already begun their digital transformation by adopting greater mobile- and cloud-based technology were probably able to make this shift with relative ease. Ironically, companies who *weren't* so prepared ultimately found the digital transformation agent they had been searching for in the form of a novel respiratory infection. The black swan event accelerated change that had to happen anyway.

## THE RED SWAN

THERE IS A quote often attributed to Mark Twain (though its true source remains anonymous). It goes:

> It ain't what you don't know that gets you in trouble. It's what you know for sure that just ain't so.

I propose we add to our thinking the red swan. The red swan refers to the things we think we know that are not actually so.

In the risk management space, part of knowing your business is acknowledging that you don't know everything. You don't know that at least 20 percent of your process and technology stack is not operating as intended or that the controls you expect to be working may not be. This idea of red swans may influence your perspective on how to plan your digital defenses.

It's human nature to think that a control you've put in place that has worked so far will continue to work over the long term. But you cannot paint a static picture of your digital landscape (a concept we'll discuss in further detail later in the book). The efficacy of controls degrades over time. This principle should be foundational in the mindset of risk-aware professionals. They have to instill in themselves a belief that approximately 20 percent of all controls are going to be broken at any point in time.

The red swans are the control checks you thought were happening, the control validations you believed were accurate, and the actions, activities, and progress you trusted were happening but weren't. Assume that 20 percent of your controls are broken—and that you need to find them. This mindset is essential for managing a digital risk program, and it pertains to your tools, processes, and even your people. You have to find a way to continuously check that 20 percent and continuously check it *differently*.

## Critical Security Controls 3 and 6: Continuous Vulnerability Management[13] and Maintenance, Monitoring, and Analysis of Audit Logs[14]

Organizations build layers of defense and they implement next-generation architecture through zero trust, but all businesses have to deal with risk exceptions or risk acceptance—deviations from your controls that you need to perform in order to achieve some business outcome.

This is where continuous vulnerability management is essential.

As your organization comes up with the top ten list of things you ought to be doing in holistic risk management, and as you begin to mature and adopt a more structured framework like that of the NIST CSCs, continuous validation must become a foundational concept.

Continuous validation was once done more manually by organizations, but it's become so important that much capital has gone into funding companies that build technology whose only job is to continuously test and validate your controls at machine speed.

This ties in directly to the concept of CSC 6, the maintenance, monitoring, and analysis of your audit logs. Consider your audit logs the key performance indicators of how the health and wellness of your organization is reconciling with the controls you *think* are working.

The combination of these two CSCs is synonymous with the concept of people, processes, and technology being used to verify

---

[13] "CIS Control 7: Continuous Vulnerability Management," Center for Internet Safety, accessed May 18, 2021, https://www.cisecurity.org/controls/continuous-vulnerability-management/.

[14] "CIS Control 6: Maintenance, Monitoring, and Analysis of Audit Logs," Center for Internet Security, accessed May 18, 2021, https://www.cisecurity.org/controls/maintenance-monitoring-and-analysis-of-audit-logs/.

> controls are working as you thought they would—not just setting
> them and forgetting them.
>     Implementing these two controls will reduce the probability of
> unfortunate surprises.

## Independent Validation

One of the best ways to test the 20 percent of your technology stack
is to bring in third parties. One of those parties can and should be
outside professional hackers.

There are three types of hackers. White hat hackers are the good
guys who work with companies to test their resources openly and
honestly. Gray hat hackers work with companies as their normal
day job, but also engage in the dark web on the side. Then there are
black hat hackers, who are truly nefarious and conduct malfeasance
for their own gain.

You enhance digital health by hiring white hat hackers to attack
your organization. This can be done using black box testing, where
you place significant limits on what the hacker can see; gray box testing, where you give the hacker a greater level of insight; or white box
testing, where you completely open your environment to be attacked
as it would be by a real threat.

You'll find that no matter how often you do this testing, something
will turn up that wasn't working as well as you thought. Red swans
will pop up all over your radar.

Not only does good internal hygiene include bringing in outsiders
to simulate attacks, but you'll also want to rotate which companies
you use to provide the service. The varied perspectives, skillsets, and

techniques that actual attackers will use to challenge your systems and processes will only add to your company's resilience.

For example, some attackers will leverage social media to trick end users into clicking on phishing emails. Others will stand up websites that look legitimate and use them to craft an email from the CEO to the CFO, telling them to quickly wire a certain amount of money as part of an urgent acquisition or some other type of business transaction. These are known as business email compromises, and they are so artfully crafted that many organizations have lost money as a result of them. They utilize effective social engineering by preying on people's fear of screwing up an order from their boss. As such, companies are losing millions.

Most companies that suffer from this sort of attack likely had technology that monitored for fraudulent emails. They might have had people monitoring those controls. But if they weren't constantly testing the controls, assuming that 20 percent of them were broken, then what they knew for sure just wasn't so.

The gold standard for email phishing protection is Domain-Based Message Authentication, Reporting, and Conformance (DMARC). DMARC is a widely used and recognized email authentication protocol. It is designed to give email domain owners the ability to protect their domain from unauthorized use, commonly known as email spoofing. Benefits of DMARC include:

1. Disallowing unauthorized use of your company's email domain name
2. Enhanced visibility into who or what is sending email using your domain name

3.  Greater brand trust due to its implementation

Employee impersonation attacks or email spoofing from outside your company are protected by DMARC. Next time an attacker tries to send a fraudulent email request from yourceo@yourcompany.com to yourcfo@yourcompany.com, it will be blocked. It is a best practice to maintain this constant testing.

If we are to stick with the email compromise example, you have to know how many money transfers you do per day. Is it ten? Or is it ten thousand? If it's ten, then you want to test a sample of those ten every couple of weeks. If it's ten thousand, you'll obviously need to increase that sample testing frequency.

It goes without saying that these types of tests contribute to operational overhead. They take time and money. You have to find ways to continuously identify all of the people involved in money transfers, be sure they have the proper training and awareness, and ensure they're periodically rotated to a different position. This rotation is of particular importance because anyone managing finances can be a target of fraud. They can also be compromised to work with someone on the outside to move money out the door. Left in the position long enough, they might even find a loophole in the system that becomes too enticing for them to resist.

At the core of the red swan concept is this:

Absolutism in the digital realm is something you need to be wary of. It causes you to create blind spots in your cyber risk management. An underlying sense of humility and skeptical inquiry are foundational elements to a pragmatic orientation.

Stay humble and hungry. Know that you don't know everything. You must continuously be learning. You must continuously be improving. You need to validate your systems and processes tirelessly in order to maintain the internal hygiene necessary to keep your digital landscape secure.

Part of this comes from a perspective of humility, not hubris. We've all heard that pride comes before the fall, but hubris in this space is deadly. If you ever find yourself saying, "We're secure, we've got this, everything is under control," then you're on a path of laziness that leads to a degradation of process and technology control efficacy that can set off a catastrophic chain of events.

Based on this concept, the industry is evolving from the sound practice of defense-in-depth to zero-trust models. While easier to adopt in cloud-based environments due to their modern infrastructure capabilities, zero trust introduces the concept of the strictest controls by not trusting any identity or asset by default, including those already inside the network perimeter.

## What Is Zero Trust?

You have to change your way of thinking when it comes to zero trust. For example, companies utilize legacy systems that have a defense and depth that they're building in the new cloud-based environments such as Amazon Web Services and Google Cloud. When doing so, it's much easier to build zero trust.

As defined in NIST Special Publication 800-207, *Zero Trust Architecture*, "Zero trust (ZT) is the term for an evolving set of cybersecurity paradigms that move defenses from static, network-based perimeters to focus on users, assets, and resources. A zero-trust architecture (ZTA) uses zero-trust principles to plan industrial and enterprise infrastructure and workflows. Zero trust assumes there is no implicit trust granted to assets or user accounts based solely on their physical or network location (i.e., local area networks versus the internet) or based on asset ownership (enterprise or personally owned)." Imagine this concept as if every system and application you run has no trust for any other system or application unless you explicitly *create* trust between them. Defense and depth as strategies are still relevant, but zero trust is the next horizon for you in the ever-growing cloud-first world.

Although zero-trust models are challenging to implement in data centers today given legacy investments and architectural postures that leverage virtual private networks (VPN), companies that wish to remain digitally competitive must do so. If you want to deliver digital transformation for your business with a cloud-first and mobile-first modern-delivery-inspired strategy, this approach will build risk insurance into that plan.

Security industry entrepreneur Jay Chaudhry, whose life story deserves its own book, has created companies solving these types of challenges. His latest company, ZScaler, is a cloud-native secure switchboard. Chaudhry's company is helping end the legacy use of VPNs with persistent connections for remote endpoints and establishing a zero-trust environment in our not-too-distant digital future.

This type of solution should be on your business roadmap.

# BACK TO COMPANY X

AS AN EXECUTIVE, you need to have a hand in establishing the proper creative tension, correct reporting structure, and appropriate amount of independence. The FCC report told us that Company X did not accomplish this. Their security team was working independently of their technology team. The controls they thought they had in place weren't being tested, validated, and didn't work as intended, which ultimately led to the breach.

This existential event for Company X is a prime example of what happens when a company *thinks* something is in place. Company X's organizational design eroded trust and communication between teams, which led them to trust controls instead—controls that ultimately failed.

What Company X knew for sure just wasn't so.

Organizational design matters when it comes to setting forth your best efforts at resilience. If you were to perform a survey today, you'd find that approximately half of all chief security officers report to chief information officers. Does this create a dynamic where, when push comes to shove, technology and the availability of technology supersede the protection of that technology?

The answer is—it depends.

Security has taken a back seat to technology delivery in the past. I would argue that the enlightened business and technology leaders of today have learned from the mistakes of the past. When big business CEOs are going on record saying that their security teams are getting a blank check, everyone gets the point. With 3.5 million open cybersecurity jobs today, the rapid digitization of our economy and finances, and the compounding threat, this priority has become obvious for all to see.

An effective organizational design is one in which the appropriate amount of creative tension occurs. Your security and risk teams should be good guardians of your organization, setting the right guardrails, and testing and protecting what the technology department is developing, whether it's building new infrastructure or developing new software.

Security needs to allow technology their independence, but also needs to be able to call out risks that are being introduced by the technology team. This can obviously be a challenge, as the technology team is likely attempting to move quickly to develop systems and applications in order to meet predetermined business needs.

As such, a common risk taxonomy needs to be developed where all stakeholders are using the same terminology with the same understanding of its meaning. That does not mean these teams will all have the same near-term delivery goals, but it does mean they need a glossary of terms they can all reference, agree on, and apply with the appropriate context and understanding.

Speaking the same language helps teams step back and look at processes end-to-end. Looking at processes end-to-end helps identify missing steps, sequencing friction, and good old-fashioned process gaps that help restructure your approach for more effective and streamlined delivery.

This is where standardization based on industry-recognized bodies such as the NIST Critical Security Controls helps technologists, security professionals, and organizations come to a common understanding of their world.

For example, if you are onboarding software, at some point along the line you must look more deeply into the functionality and potential risks that software is introducing. If risks are identified, the process should allow for the entire onboarding to stop. That finding should be valued as a micro-insight that could have macro-implications for your company.

Whether through software onboarding or software development, modern delivery aspirations should include a shift-left goal, which means that design controls' checks and balances should be moved further upstream before they come to your risk teams. Bad news does not age well, and time is the currency of life. The sooner you identify risks, the higher probability you have of addressing them before the costs associated with them have time to compound.

As Sun Tzu once said, "To know your enemy, you must become your enemy... If you know yourself but not the enemy, for every victory gained you will also suffer a defeat. If you know neither the enemy nor yourself, you will succumb in every battle." To outwit the devil, you have to think like one.

The known knowns that just aren't so are assumptions that prove incorrect. So, how do you validate that all that you believe is happening is actually occurring? You must instill in yourself the discipline, rigor, and pursuit of process excellence to answer the perpetual questions:

What assumptions have I made?

What assumptions are others making?

How do we reduce the potential negative impact of those assumptions?

What do I know and who needs to know what I know?

Consistently seeking answers to these questions helps you both double-check your own thinking as well as expedites communication across what can be the fog of digital war. Asking these questions helps eliminate the assumptions that may be occurring between yourself and other decision makers in the digital security space.

chapter six

# NAPOLEON AT AUSTERLITZ AND THE DYNAMIC RISK LANDSCAPE

*In victory, you deserve champagne;*
*in defeat, you need it.*

—Napoleon Bonaparte (1769–1821)

NAPOLEON FAMOUSLY STATED THAT ONE SHOULD NEVER paint a picture of the battlefield because a picture is static. It doesn't change. A battlefield is dynamic and ever-changing, and Napoleon employed a successful strategy at the Battle of Austerlitz, one that ties directly to this concept of static and dynamic environments.

Napoleon was an innovator. One such innovation was to take his monolithic army and break it up into smaller corps to "march divided but strike united." Napoleon first used the *corps d'armée* in 1805, a military innovation that provided Napoleon with a significant battlefield advantage, especially early on. The corps was designed to be an independent military group containing cavalry, artillery, and infantry that was capable of defending against a numerically superior foe. The corps enabled the bulk of Napoleon's forces to penetrate into a weak section of enemy lines without risking his own communications or flank.

In awe of his capabilities and innovations, other European armies gradually adopted this approach. The corps has remained an integral feature of French Army organization to this day.

The corps allowed Napoleon's troops to move around roads and across terrain independently and then meet up later at a certain juncture. When Napoleon did this at Austerlitz, he added an additional strategy—he feigned a weak right flank.

By feigning, Napoleon positioned his troops to make his right flank appear weaker than it actually was. Using the mists that had covered the battlefield, he positioned troops to reinforce this supposedly weak corps, unbeknownst to his enemy.

Feigning weakness equates to a false retreat in many ways, a strategy utilized by the Mongolians in their rule of Asia and parts of Europe. The Mongolians would attack their enemy, then retreat, pretending that they had been hurt and were on the run and thus drawing the opposition into a trap.

Napoleon did the same at Austerlitz. He drew in the Russian and Austrian troops using the change in the weather and terrain. His opposition felt assured of victory, only to meet up with a mass of troops who had not been weakened. This strategy eventually helped Napoleon win the battle.

## Critical Security Control 7: Email and Web Browser Protections[15]

Armies throughout history have used the tactic of flanking. They try to take advantage of the soft spot in the line, which is the flank.

The flank of your organization is your email and web browsers. While web browsers were once the most targeted to compromise the endpoints in an organization, email phishing has been there in

---

[15] "CIS Control 9: Email and Web Browser Protections," Center for Internet Security, accessed May 18, 2021, https://www.cisecurity.org/controls/email-and-web-browser-protections/.

the background. Now phishing is being used to leverage social engineering and knowledge-based authentication.

If you factor in a risk-based approach, prioritizing the higher probability and impact outcomes that cause organizational hazards, it is crucial that you double down on your controls in the email and web browser space, solutions that act like a TSA agent on email coming in and out of your organization. A TSA agent examines packages going in and out of the airport, and there are certain email protectionary services that offer the same level of control. Domain-Based Message Authentication, Reporting, and Conformance (DMARC), mentioned earlier, will further complement this layer of control.

As it pertains to your web browsers, you also must ensure that you're using current secure versions of web browsers and not the ones that have the highest risks associated with them. It is also necessary that they route to the internet through proxies that behave like secured switchboard operators. There are some legacy browsers still in use that are frequently exploited and, as such, should not be allowed in your environment.

## DON'T PAINT A PICTURE

WHEN IT COMES to cyber warfare, you cannot paint a static picture.

Without hyperbole, cyber warfare occurs twenty-four hours a day, 365 days per year, whether it's being fought by a person sitting behind a keyboard working for a criminal gang or a nation-state or if it's being waged by automated bots and software constantly scanning and trying to infect machines.

The knowledge that this battlefield is constantly changing enhances the foundational concept that the efficacy of controls degrades over time—which is why it is critical that you stay vigilant when it comes to your digital risk management, including your technical controls, managerial controls, procedural controls, process controls—the list goes on. A control should reduce the inherent gross risk to a residual net risk that is within the tolerance levels of your business.

Companies can no longer consider themselves robust or unbreakable. Doing so lends credence to the idea that they don't need to change. A number of years ago, a major software company ran an advertisement stating that their software was indeed unbreakable. This, of course, incentivized hackers to prove them wrong—and they did.

No one—again, *no one*—can be perfectly resilient to cyberattacks, as validated by data breaches we read about in the news every day. You cannot simply aspire to be resilient (meaning how well you can defend against and recover quickly from an attack and the pace and efficiency with which you protect, detect, and correct). You must also work to become anti-fragile. You want to gain from the disorder.

This means building beyond the defense-in-depth model or layers of defense. Those layers of defense must be constantly checked and validated through continuous validation so that you're actually getting the defense you expected—but you can also deploy a constant feigning of weakness while your second horizon begins adopting zero-trust characteristics. You do this by putting in your environment systems and servers that are unpatched and essentially unloved and uncared for so that they are actually more easily compromised by an attacker.

# HONEYPOTS AND THE DECEPTION LAYER OF DEFENSE

YOU'RE LIKELY ASKING, "Why on earth would I do that?"

If an attacker is trying to break into your environment, they're looking for a foothold. They're looking for a system that they can use to move laterally within your environment.

To combat this, you can place what is commonly known as honeypots, or systems that don't have the same level of security controls and aren't patched as effectively so they can be more easily compromised by attackers. Doing this allows you to more actively monitor what they're doing, placing *you* in greater control of the situation.

## The System Administration Network Security Institute

As mentioned earlier, I credit the SANS Institute for driving technical security development in the last thirty-plus years. SANS was co-founded by Steven Northcutt. I had the privilege of getting to know him roughly twenty years ago.

Steven would say things like, "You need to know your network and how this translates to the concept of know thyself." He would tell me how I would need to sit and watch, for days on end, my intrusion detection systems and look at the traffic patterns, like the lines of code in *The Matrix*. Watching this traffic was a behavior desirable in more sophisticated defenders.

Steven also talked about the concept of the honeypot and how one of his disciples was the grandfather of the honeypot strategy later codified by Lance Spitzer.

It was then that the light bulb went off—when Steven and the SANS team talked about concepts that related to my idea of "know thyself." It was also one of the first instances when I saw how world history can parallel the strategies and tactics critical to cybersecurity today.

In the layered defense model, consider this your deception layer. Honeypots have been used for many years for various research initiatives to understand how malicious software behaves and what techniques attackers use.

This strategy not only allows you to observe but to cut the attackers off if necessary and perhaps even assign attributions. One of the hardest things to do in cybersecurity is to assign attributions to an attack. Attributions means identifying who is actually executing the attack. Feigning weakness and drawing in the enemy potentially gives you the time to make those identifications. Be aware this is an investment most organizations are not able to perform.

If you're an organizational executive who might not be as familiar with these strategies, you may be asking yourself what you can and cannot safely put in these honeypots such that if they do come under attack, you keep your risk profile low.

The answer is to use synthetic data. For example, let's imagine an attacker is looking for privately identifiable information, say an end user's name, social security number, and date of birth; credit card information; bank information; or intellectual property you're developing. Your team can create synthetic data that looks like any of the above—but isn't actually said data.

The team can then place that data into an unpatched and unprotected server and label it as sensitive private information, or any other name that would draw the interest of an attacker. Even if the data is lost from the honeypot as a result of the attack, you won't care, because it's garbage data.

The idea of honeypots isn't a new one, but not all organizations use them. You're more likely to see them being used by a team that has moved up the maturity curve, one that is no longer focused only on defense. They're actively searching the environment for other threats and vulnerabilities.

## DON'T SET IT AND FORGET IT: VERSION 2.0

THE MORE RISK exceptions/acceptances you introduce into your environment, the faster your controls ossify. They become more brittle, breakable, and less dependable. The more you introduce these exceptions to control standards, the more you age your company and dilute the effectiveness of your organizational immunity and resiliency. We check our heart rate, blood pressure, temperature, and perform a wide range of biological health checks. We test how quickly we can raise our heart rate, how quickly it slows down after strain—the list of physical health checks goes on and on.

We need a similar mindset when measuring our security effectiveness. Since at least the seventeenth century, the scientific method has been an empirical method of acquiring knowledge that has characterized the development of science, involving careful observation and applying rigorous skepticism about what is observed, given that cognitive assumptions can distort how one interprets the observation.

The scientific method has five basic steps, plus one feedback step:

1. Make an observation.
2. Ask a question.
3. Form a hypothesis or testable explanation.
4. Make a prediction based on the hypothesis.
5. Test the prediction.
6. Iterate: use the results to make new hypotheses or predictions.

We can apply this to security:

➤ Observation: a cyber risk is present, and we have built defenses to protect our business.

➤ Question: how quickly has the security operations center picked up the attack?

➤ Hypothesis: based on our investments, we would detect it immediately.

➤ Prediction: based on the hypothesis that we would immediately detect it, we predict we can effectively respond and eliminate the threat within sixty minutes.

➤ Test the prediction: simulating an attack, measure when the attack was accurately detected and the threat was effectively eliminated.

> Iterate: was it effectively addressed in sixty minutes? If yes, good. See if you can reduce that timeline. If not, take corrective measures and test again.

The same logic may be applied in a more granular fashion with the following questions:

> How accurately were the issues diagnosed?
> How quickly were those issues routed to an incident responder?
> How effectively did the incident responder analyze the ticket?
> How rapidly did the responder get to the appropriate endpoint?

That last point is critical.

In medicine, there is the concept of the golden hour. If you can get to a hospital emergency room within sixty minutes of sustaining a life-threatening injury, you have a higher probability of surviving; with each minute that passes, that probability decreases.

The same holds true in cybersecurity.

Often, if you can get on an endpoint within sixty minutes of the attack, you have a higher probability of containing the contagion, so to speak, and keeping it from exploiting the hardware and moving laterally within your environment.

The point is that it's not enough to create honeypots and leave them be. You cannot paint a static picture. Layering your defense does not mean that you can simply set your protections and forget it. You must exercise continuous testing and validation—even for your honeypots with garbage data.

Validation exercises were once manual, but they're so useful and necessary that it's now wise to invest in solutions that do it for us.

There is an entire continuous validation cybersecurity space where you can purchase a software solution that constantly runs attacks on your network, validating the efficacy of your controls and essentially answering the scientific method questions posed above.

Software like this used to be a nice-to-have—it's now a must-have in terms of validating your security hygiene. If honeypots become a part of your strategy, then you also must include a cycle that periodically refreshes the synthetic data you've created.

However, whether you're a part of a younger large company, a startup, or an established organization with a legacy mindset, you need to have the honeypot concept on your roadmap.

Once again, recent news would suggest that you allocate approximately 8 to 18 percent of your total technology spend on digital defense. Keep in mind, though, that budget is an input while successful security risk management is an outcome akin to your health. If you don't have your health, you don't have anything in life. Likewise, if your organization does not have the security integrity of its assets, it may not be left with anything at all. If your startup consists of you and one other person in your garage starting a cloud-native company, then you probably don't have the resources to do this. But if you're a legacy organization that's serious about digital risk management, then you must, at the very least, get the fundamentals right.

This means investing in a security risk leader and a team of professionals. Invest in technology, allocate a portion of your technology budget to security, and develop the correct processes for building a security operations team, a response team, and a forensics team.

This isn't to say that smaller organizations don't have options. A fifty-person company may have a few information technology employees with at least one of them spending part of their time managing your digital security. They would prioritize that time by making sure there is an investment in controls that protect the organization. So, if you're a cloud-based company, you'll want to subscribe to cloud-based solutions that will provide firewall protection, remote access, malware detection, and the traditional virus-scanning solutions we all have on our laptops but that are also extended to the cloud.

Large cloud service providers now offer services that you simply subscribe to instead of having to purchase all the hardware and software. Smaller companies utilizing these services can leverage what is called technical debt. Some systems and applications are older than others, meaning that they can lag behind on patching and upgrades. If you're a smaller organization, you can decide that those technical debts can be leveraged as your honeypots—consciously forego upgrading these systems but place them in a secured zone in your network where you can monitor whether or not they end up compromised.

If you're a larger organization with the budget to match, your big buckets are protecting, detecting, and correcting—meaning that of that 18 percent, you'll likely spend approximately 60 percent on protecting, about 30 percent on detecting, and maybe 10 percent on correcting. It is a sophisticated step to take, but a more mature organization can get a higher return on investment as a result.

This is so because security in a large number of companies adopts a checkbox mindset—they set it and forget it. They paint a static picture and base their defense on that picture. We now know that isn't an effective strategy. We must acknowledge and take advantage of the changing terrain, resetting both our defense and our plan of attack accordingly.

Things go wrong and you need to execute in the absence of hope that someone else is going to come to your rescue. In most cases, you're on your own, though you might go so far as to hire a digital forensics company or some other third-party service to help you.

You need to develop a mentality and self-sustainability similar to the army corps that Napoleon developed such that you're able to protect and defend yourself when help isn't available. Know that there will be days that you drink to celebrate and days that you drink to drown your sorrows, and you'll be operating with a self-awareness that can be devastatingly absent in this space.

# chapter seven

# THE BATTLE OF WATERLOO AND THE NATURE OF BAD DECISIONS

*A strong character is one
that will not be unbalanced by the
most powerful emotions.*

—Carl von Clausewitz (1780–1831), *On War*

P RUSSIAN GENERAL AND MILITARY THEORIST CARL VON
Clausewitz took his learnings from the Napoleonic wars and
compiled them into his book, *On War*. In it, he highlighted
the concept of the fog of war—how difficult it is to make clear, well-
thought-out decisions in the thick of battle.

There is this same fog when it comes to fighting cyber war.

In both physical and digital battle, the fog comes in the form of
VUCA—volatility, uncertainty, complexity, and ambiguity. It is something battlefield commanders have faced, and it is something we
encounter today in the domain of cyber risk management. VUCA
clouds judgment, causes significant mental and physical fatigue, and
leads to poor execution and decision making. As such, we must ask
ourselves what we can learn from history to help us make better choices
in the face of VUCA.

If you begin to abandon the principles that you know are important
in cyber warfare, it can lead to unfortunate outcomes. You can crumble
under the weight of human stress, fatigue, poor decision-making, and
the degradation of the efficacy of controls.

We know that Napoleon is widely regarded as one of the greatest, if
not *the* greatest tactical commander of all time. His situational awareness, improvisation, understanding of the battlefield, and ability to
shift gears were remarkable.

But at Waterloo, something changed.

Heavy rain had fallen the night before and made the field quite muddy. Normally, Napoleon took the initiative and launched his battle attacks early, typically in the early hours of the morning, and surprised his enemy with aggression. But this time he did not. Historians argue that he waited until he thought the field had hardened so he could more easily move his cannon around. His hesitancy has been a point of speculation ever since.

Was it battle fatigue? Was Napoleon already experiencing symptoms of the stomach cancer that many believe eventually killed him like his sister before him? Or had he succumbed to a life lived on the battlefield? Whatever the case, Napoleon's power of mentalization appears to have abandoned him.

Napoleon was behaving in a manner uncommon for him. He was neither decisive nor resolute. He did not display his usual aggression, and he launched the battle later in the day. As the timing played out, the army he sent off to fight with the Prussians and keep them at bay didn't find them because the Prussians were already on the way to reinforce the English, led by the Duke of Wellington.

The battle ensued and the English took a defensive position. They placed flankers in three different large farmhouses that proved difficult to break into, and wave after wave of French attacks were repulsed by the English. Napoleon knew that timing would be important and that if he didn't address the issue quickly, the day would be lost when the Prussians arrived.

Now, after already having hesitated, after letting fatigue and his possible ailment erode his decision quality, Napoleon became exasperated and attempted the equivalent of a Hail Mary. He ordered Marshal Ney (the bravest man in the world, so named by Napoleon) to launch an unsupported attack on the British with his cavalry. This meant Napoleon wasn't set up properly to open the attack with his cannons, and he didn't have his infantry troops positioned and ready to provide support.

Ney led the gallop to what he *hoped* would be glory.

The British fell into the "square," a technique where they lined up in large squares reinforced by lines within lines. They repulsed wave after wave of cavalry attacks—and broke the French spirit. The cavalry was turned back with huge losses on their side. As the sun set, so did the French hope of victory. The horizon began to darken not only with dusk, but with the dark outline of black-clad Prussian troops coming to reinforce the British side.

At the height of desperation, Napoleon sent in his Old Guard—and they were subsequently wiped out. In fact, the last of the Old Guard formed their own square as they were surrounded by the Duke of Wellington. The duke graciously offered them a chance to surrender, but they rebuked him with profanity and were wiped out to the last man.

Napoleon was captured shortly thereafter and sent away for the rest of his life. Ultimately, he died on the island of Saint Helena off the coast of Africa.

## Critical Security Controls 5, 11, and 12: Secure Configuration for Hardware and Software on Mobile Devices;[16] Secure Configuration for Network Devices Such as Firewalls, Routers and Switches;[17] and Boundary Defense[18]

Wellington hardened and solidified the defense of his assets by using the farmhouses Napoleon attacked to protect his troops. Similarly, he used the British square to defend against the cavalry.

Sometimes organizations don't leverage the strengths they have. If you've followed the CSCs discussed so far, you know your assets and inventory, but you don't want to allocate a large number of "troops" to an already well-secured "farmhouse."

Beyond asset inventory, you want to spend time hardening your servers, applications, endpoints, network devices, firewalls, switches, and IoT devices. But, after that, you must acknowledge the fact that you've achieved a certain level of hardening (and validate it) so that you can channel your defenses to the other soft areas in your network.

You need to have the right horses for the right courses. Wellington employed various methods of hardening his defense depending on the attack. As a defender, you need to do the same

---

[16] "CIS Control 5: Secure Configuration for Hardware and Software on Mobile Devices, Laptops, Workstations and Servers," Center for Internet Security, accessed May 18, 2021, https://www.cis ecurity.org/controls/secure-configuration-for-hardware-and-software-on-mobile-devices-laptops -workstations-and-servers/.

[17] "CIS Control 11: Secure Configuration for Network Devices, Such as Firewalls, Routers and Switches," Center for Internet Security, accessed May 18, 2021, https://www.cisecurity.org/controls /secure-configuration-for-network-devices-such-as-firewalls-routers-and-switches/.

[18] "CIS Control 12: Boundary Defense," Center for Internet Security, accessed May 18, 2021, https:// www.cisecurity.org/controls/boundary-defense/.

in order to reduce the probability and location of where things can go wrong. You must harden all the channels in your network, including your mobile devices, laptops, and workstations.

Firewalls, routers, and switches are also attack vectors that need to be hardened according to best practices. It's additionally important to know that when your vulnerabilities become apparent—when there's a new malware such as a self-propagating worm—you need to revisit those devices that are susceptible to that type of attack in order to harden them and adjust their formation against those types of attacks.

If you do not explicitly require a technology feature or service to be turned on, turn it off. It's that simple. If you need a technology feature or service turned on, allowed, or somehow enabled, have a clear business justification documenting that decision.

## OODA

WE ARE ALL human.

We all feel fatigue and exhaustion. When we feel a sense of urgency compounded by fatigue and exhaustion, it erodes the quality of our decisions, particularly when it comes to what we think we know for sure.

Time and time again, incident responders in companies trying to defend themselves against sophisticated attackers go off-script during a cyberattack. It's human nature to feel fear and pressure, to try to make quick decisions that you think will address the near-term problem instead of following the plan—the tactics you created in times of decreased stress. Decision quality erodes with stress and fatigue.

Whether for pandemic continuity incidents or for cybersecurity incidents, responders begin to make poor decisions as the stress level increases. It is critical, once again, to know thyself—to fall back on the plan and the key principles that you believe in, no matter what. In good times and in bad, you must hold to the truth of that plan, one that has a process flow, that has the balance of disciplined execution, but allows for creative improvisation in the face of ambiguity.

The OODA Loop is a set of tools that we can add to our belt developed by the United States Air Force. OODA stands for:

> Observe
> Orient
> Decide
> Act

This four-step approach to decision-making focuses on filtering the available information and putting it into context. From there, you quickly make the most appropriate decision while also understanding that changes can be made as more data becomes available.

We deal with imperfect information constantly, half wrong and half incorrect. In the face of VUCA, the OODA Loop acts as a set of tried-and-true principles of a tactical sort of protection for your organization. Those principals come together in the face of stressful scenarios.

Say you experience a midnight attack on your infrastructure by a cybercriminal, a pandemic, or an earthquake. In any of these scenarios, you will leverage the muscle memory built from reading through those plans (out loud because we skip over things when we read in our head) ahead of time and practicing those plans you've developed.

Then, you factor in the other teams at your disposal to manage VUCA using the OODA Loop for a rapidly evolving tactical scenario that requires both reorientation and continuous streams of information.

This muscle memory combined with instinctual situational awareness creates a mindset that becomes a fundamental aspect of your team's digital weapons defense systems. This mindset is also what differentiates the amateurs from the professionals. (For greater insights on amateurs versus professionals, I invite you to explore the mental models blog Farnam Street (FS) at https://fs.blog/start/.)

## System 1 and System 2

In the 1970s, noted psychologists Daniel Kahneman and Amos Tversky researched people's thought process in making decisions. Based on their analysis, they found that decision quality erodes over the course of time when it comes to certain types of decisions. They broke the concept down into two systems.

System 1 is a portion of your brain that doesn't need to be taxed when making decisions. These decisions can be quickly and easily made from the biological RAM in your brain where information is readily available—the sky is blue, one plus one is two. You don't have to think. You just know the answer.

This is where situational awareness resides—seeing possibilities balanced with probabilities. Napoleon spoke of this as "a gift of being able to see at a glance the possibilities of the terrain." In Lawrence Freedman's all-time epic book on strategic thinking, *Strategy: A History*, he cites genius as "a combination of rational and subrational intellectual and emotional faculties that make up intuition."

System 2, on the other hand, is for problems too complicated or complex for System 1. It requires thought and analysis. You have a good deal less System 2 capacity than you do System 1. This is where System 1 judgments are processed and turned into long-term plans or strategies. System 2 requires more time and energy and taxes you mentally and emotionally.

In their examination, Kahneman and Tversky observed a pattern in prison probation panels. Inmates that came in for their hearings before noon had a much higher probability of being discharged or paroled than those coming later in the afternoon. They found that as the parole boards thought through each case, they were exhausting their System 2 capabilities. After lunch, they were so tired of making decisions that they made them in haste and defaulted to saying "no."

Why does Jeff Bezos schedule his most important meetings at ten in the morning? Why do so many leaders make sure their most important decisions are made in the morning? Whether consciously or unconsciously, they understand that the quality of their decisions erodes as the day goes on.

As Napoleon's incredible System 1 generated a backlog of ideas adapting to circumstances to be managed in System 2, it began to tax his assertiveness and the quality of his decisions. He hoped to skip over the hard part of taking the farmhouses and simply ride around them and crush the British with his cavalry. Napoleon failed. The Duke of Wellington's discipline in hardening the farmhouses, forming squares when necessary, and simply fighting a defense battle aimed at delaying the French goal of a quick victory led to his ultimate success.

You do want to attract great System 1 thinking into your business resilience strategy by attracting creative thinkers. As security evolves, the technology and/or law enforcement background typical of a security team will also draw on diverse perspectives that will strengthen the members' core skillset and the team as a whole. For example, I have hired professionals who began their careers in math, literature, science, and music before moving into security. Those individuals grew into security professionals with a well-rounded perspective.

However, you also need to understand the burn rate as it applies to your business's System 2 thinkers. Sound strategic thinking takes time and effort. You won't be able to buy a business risk strategy for your organization off the shelf.

A bespoke and thoughtful effort is required in hardening the known-known assets, understanding the relational interplay of those systems, and understanding the unique pivot-point risks these relationships have. Remember, every network is its own snowflake, similar to, yet different, than all of the others.

Speaking of which...

# chapter eight

# SNOWFLAKES THAT COMPOUND INTO SNOWBALLS AND THE BATTLE OF GETTYSBURG

*Big things have small beginnings.*

—T. E. Lawrence, also known as
Lawrence of Arabia (1888–1935)

# D
ID YOU EVER HEAR THIS GROWING UP?

*For lack of a nail, a horseshoe was lost.*
*For lack of a horseshoe, a horse was lost.*
*For lack of a horse, a rider was lost.*

*For lack of a rider, a message was lost.*
*For lack of a message, a battle was lost.*
*For lack of a battle, a war was lost.*
*For lack of war, a kingdom was lost.*

While you need to maintain a level head and be a calm guardian for your organization, you also need to be aware that small things can manifest themselves into big outcomes—life-changing outcomes, whether for you or for your company.

During the American Civil War, the South won the Battle of Chancellorsville under General Lee in what was a high-water mark for the South. The North was in a dilemma. They had been losing battles to the more experienced Southern army while Lee had his greatest victory to date. Abraham Lincoln had changed generals several times and assigned Ulysses S. Grant as head of the Northern armies.

The dynamics were changing. The South had the advantage.

Then one day, a group of Northern troops was on patrol when they came across a band of Southern rebels. A skirmish ensued. The

Northern troops were on a hill, and between them and the Southern troops was a large picket fence. Over the course of days, the skirmish developed into a massive battle because both Lee and Grant began allocating more and more troops to the fight.

Ultimately, that skirmish turned into the Battle of Gettysburg, the turning point of the American Civil War.

You should be aware of the fact that a small skirmish changed the tide of the Civil War because there were a number of different, seemingly lesser, historical key points to remember.

The North had recently deployed a new rifle that allowed for more rapid-fire shooting. Technological innovation played a role in this outcome. Understanding how technology is evolving and potentially shifting the landscape of the battlefield is important.

The North had the higher ground. Compare that with how you position yourself in the marketplace. The fence between the Northern and Southern troops was critical because wave after wave of seasoned rebels charged up that hill and then had to climb over the fence, which got them shot to pieces. That fence served as the moat that protected the Northern forces and gave them the advantage. Similarly, you should have a "moat" in place for your organization, whether to protect against digital threats or competitors.

We can also learn from this concept of big things with small beginnings that no security incident is too small to be considered.

A single infection on a laptop should not be disregarded because it may grow. It can propagate and infect other assets. It might be a landing spot for an attacker who's using it for lateral transfer to other endpoints.

This is why protect-detect-correct should apply to both big things like broad cyberattacks and small things such as minor infections in your organization. It's not that you should play Chicken Little and run around exclaiming that the sky is falling. Not everything needs to be treated as a high-severity priority number one. It's that everything should be addressed in some formal fashion. That infection might be a priority number four, meaning you have some time to get to it, but you need to account for your entire ecosystem. What matters is that it's on the list.

You need to understand key trends facing assets for which you are accountable, and you need to have a plan—even if it's a plan for a plan—to address all of your digital investments.

Are infections growing, slowing, or flat? More sophisticated programs measure the average number of security incidents per day, week, and month. Once a trend is established, thresholds above and below the statistical mean can be established. Preestablished percentages on the deviation from that mean—say 20 percent per month—allow you to measure if there is an unacceptable rise in incidents that break the top threshold and need to be investigated. If incidents drop to more than 20 percent of normal, is that because there are fewer attacks occurring, or are your monitoring solutions not detecting the actual attacks?

Further measurements can be introduced, such as the mean time to the detection of an event, the mean time to identifying and analyzing the asset in question, and the mean time to resolve the issue.

# Critical Security Control 13: Data Protection[19]

The way in which you store, collect, process, transmit, and monitor your data is essential for your organization.

There are solutions commonly referred to as data loss protection solutions. In some cases, they can be used to protect data specifically from leaving your organization, but what is more meaningful and insightful is to see how people are using your data.

How are they moving it around your network and why? What are the underlying processes?

CSC 13 relates to the processes and tools used to prevent data exfiltration and to mitigate the effects should there be an exfiltration. There are technologies that will tell you if organizational data is leaving. When you're made aware, you must become a process analyst and apply the Lean Six Sigma concept of the Five Whys. For example:

- **Question:** why did the control not detect the issue?
- **Answer:** it was not tuned correctly.

- **Question:** why was it not tuned correctly?
- **Answer:** the control operator made an error.

- **Question:** why did the operator make an error?
- **Answer:** the operator had not been trained and tested on their ability to tune the control.

- **Question:** why had the operator not been trained and tested on their ability to tune the control?

---

[19] "CIS Control 3: Data Protection," Center for Internet Security, accessed May 18, 2021, https://www.cisecurity.org/controls/data-protection/.

- **Answer:** this requirement had been descoped from the delivery of the original control to save on budget and delivery date.

- **Question:** why had these been descoped?
- **Answer:** the application of strict adherence to delivery on all original project deliverables is not being followed.

As you can see, failure to manage a business process upstream contributes to the root cause of failure of control downstream.

By asking these questions, you can understand that there's a higher return on investment in not just putting up the protections, controlling the barriers and guardrails, but also in performing process analyses to get to the root cause of a problem to move it upstream.

A concept that applies to secure software development is shifting left—making sure that developers understand well the code they're writing and reducing the probability of security vulnerabilities; but also moving it up within your organization so that good technology hygiene is factored into your technology investments.

If you allocate your energy to adding controls to protect a bad process, you'll inevitably see a regression to the mean, meaning the process at the control will wear and tear. Instead, shift your focus to the process and the architecture, correct the root cause, and reduce the process friction as the priority.

## THE NEW OIL

IF DATA IS the new oil, then, like oil in its rawest form, data needs to be refined to obtain other beneficial insights.

Oil needs to be extracted from the ground, then transported via rail cars, trucks, tanker vessels, and through pipelines. It arrives at plant refineries where crude oil is transformed into petroleum products that fuel our world.

Refining breaks crude oil down into its various components, which are then selectively reconfigured into new products. Petroleum refineries are complex and expensive industrial facilities. All refineries have three basic steps: separation, conversion, and treatment. During the refining process, crude oil is cultivated to produce different petroleum products like gasoline, diesel, and jet fuel.

This process applies to how you think of your data and its safeguarding.

Data should be collected at the source and transferred to its own refinery known as a security incident event manager (SIEM) (or any other next-generation version of an SIEM). Then the data is converted into information, the information is refined into insights and analytics by a security operations center (SOC), and the SOC analysts use that to take action and respond.

Meaningful data analytics are similar to alchemy. You take raw data, the equivalent of the metal lead, and, using predefined rules, machine-learning formulas, and the umbrella of AI solutions, convert that data lead into information gold loaded with deep-rooted value.

The philosophers' stone is a legendary substance that could reputedly turn base metals like iron and lead into gold. Sir Isaac Newton, easily the father of modern science, revolutionized our understanding of the world. Newton gave us new theories on gravity, planetary motion, and optics. He was also a devoted alchemist determined to use what he thought was his discovery of the philosopher's stone to convert lead into gold. This ancient pursuit of transmutation from lead to gold is analogous to the conversion of data into information, and the magical moment that information turns into insights.

## THE HUNDRED COINS

*It's in your moments of decision that your destiny is shaped.*
—Tony Robbins, motivational speaker (1960–)

IF YOU'RE A business leader in charge of allocating investments in resilience, having to worry about all of these little things probably sounds like an expensive proposition. But it's not about worrying—it's about awareness.

Prioritization is a fundamental aspect of risk management. You've got a system that has all of your core IP, value at risk, and financials. You should have a more regular health check on *that* rather than an endpoint that isn't as meaningful. However, you should be aware of the endpoints of the server, the database, and the workstation.

You might only check in on that endpoint on a quarterly basis, but you have a prioritized risk-based view of your world, which eliminates worry. You're not worrying as much about a single database as the core application, but you are aware of them and of the potential interweaving of disruptions that one can cause the other.

There is a great exercise called the hundred coins.

To protect a single database of noncritical data costs one coin, and you've got hundreds of coins. How do you allocate them?

A simple, visual way to answer this question is to draw a triangle. The top third has the most key information for the organization — its intellectual property, its financials, its privately identifiable data. The next third of the triangle has information that is less important but still confidential. The bottom third is publicly available data, the things that you care about but don't necessarily care if someone else has access to it.

Now draw another triangle inverse to the first. The top third of the triangle is now the largest part. That's the amount of protection that you should be applying to the tip of your information triangle, and so on as you move down. This exercise helps you visualize tiering and how to structure your awareness so that you are allocating more of your resources to the smaller, finite number of things that you care about.

## SOMETHING YOU KNOW, SOMETHING YOU HAVE, AND SOMETHING YOU ARE

HOW DO YOU eat an elephant? One bite at a time.

Where do you start, though?

When you visit the doctor, they look at your vitals, and, with about ten different measured areas, get a fairly good idea of your biological health.

With good cyber risk management and digital defenses, there are a number of questions you can ask yourself to get the same sense of your cyber health.

- Are you allocating some portion of your technology budget to protecting that technology?
- Do you have people dedicated to protecting that technology?
- Do you have a leader accountable for the activity going on in this space?
- Do you have protective controls, detective controls, and corrective controls?
- Do you periodically have someone who isn't part of your organization come and test how you're doing and give you your own health check?
- Do you acknowledge that, even with this effort, you will have blind spots in your security posture?
- Do you actually do something with that health check and are you applying the common best practices?

That last question of best practices is of particular importance.

If you're going to have an interface with the big bad internet where everything goes down, are you relying on single usernames and passwords, which we know are an old-fashioned way to authenticate individuals? Or are you applying the common best practice known as multi-factor authentication (MFA)?

MFAs are something that you know, something that you have, and something that you are—meaning, you put in your username, you type in a password, and then a text message comes to you. You then type the contents of that text message into the authenticating channel.

There are a number of different MFAs. If you do online banking, you probably use some version of multifactor authentication. It's been required for the last ten-plus years for those channels. MFA as part of your game plan is a foundational health component to consider, and if you're not employing it as a best practice, I'd advise you to start immediately.

When it comes to your personal health, if you're not exercising, the first step is to start walking. Just moving makes a difference. You can take it up from there with the right diet and an increasing level of intensity in your exercise. Cyber health is no different. Even if you don't have good answers to your health questionnaire, even if you're not doing the equivalent of walking, plan to walk. Make it part of your strategy. Have a conversation at a town hall about what is important for your organization. How do you get started on prioritizing? If you have IP, what is it and where is it? Incorporate that into your culture and strategy.

You've got health and wellness programs for your employees, right? Have one for your organization as well.

As a business leader, these are just some of the high-level questions you can start conversations with, no matter what level of maturity your company. You can be just two people starting out in a garage wanting an online presence needing best practices to adopt. Or you could be the CEO of a global financial institution that has unlimited money allocated to cybersecurity. No matter what, you must constantly interrogate yourself to determine the level of your digital health.

For business leaders that are also on corporate boards, the National Association of Corporate Directors (NACD) publishes insightful research on questions the board of directors should be asking about their organization's cybersecurity posture. For more details, see: www. nacdonline.org.

# CHECKLISTS

*No wise pilot, no matter how great his talent
and experience, fails to use a checklist.*

—Charlie Munger (1924–),
Vice Chairman, Berkshire Hathaway

EFFECTIVE RISK MANAGEMENT, whether in cybersecurity or otherwise, is not attained purely through checklists. In fact, check-the-box security is ineffective and should set off internal alarms for seasoned professionals. A balance between performance and conformance should always be on an organization's radar. Having said that, there is a time and place for checklists.

For example, the B-17 bomber almost didn't make it into flight in World War II because on its first takeoff with a very experienced crew of pilots it crashed, killing some of those pilots. The event almost put Boeing out of business. When they researched what might have happened, they realized that the mechanisms were too complicated —there were just too many steps for the pilots to go through.

Another group of pilots then got together to develop a lengthy, in-depth checklist of steps necessary to get the B-17 off the ground. Once the pilots put that checklist into use, it reduced human error and increased the probability of flight. In the end, the B-17 was able to fly and later contributed significantly to the war effort.

This checklist approach applies to medicine as well. Hospitals around the world have varying degrees of infection rates. Studies have found that when doctors go through a series of checklists, mortality rates go down. The act of going through these checklists reduces the probability of medical errors that can lead to inflammation and infection.

There are checklists you can develop for your organizations that reduce internal inflammation, to reduce as greatly as possible the amount of human error introduced into the process.

The important thing to understand when it comes to human error is that humans are consistently inconsistent. If you were to give an employee a list of one hundred questions on a topic that they knew well, they might answer with 90 percent accuracy. Asked the same questions again as time went on, but with a change in order and structure, you would see a 20 percent deviation in either direction—they might get 20 percent more answers right or 20 percent more wrong.

Why? Well, we're human.

We might have had a good night's sleep or a bad one. Maybe traffic slowed our arrival to work. Maybe we didn't have a good breakfast. Maybe we were or weren't getting along with our loved ones.

All of this comes into play when we make decisions.

Referring back to the NACD guidance on cybersecurity, here is a checklist[20] of questions business leaders and boards may wish to consider asking their security leaders. Note: the link listed in the footnote will take you to the full document, but NACD requires membership in order to view.

---

[20] "NACD," NACD, accessed May 18, 2021, https://www.nacdonline.org/.

# Ten Questions for a Board Member
# to Ask About Cybersecurity

## TIER ONE. *Policy and Governance*

How is personally identifiable information (PII) treated domestically and internationally? What are the safeguards of stolen equipment?

How many third parties have access to your systems, and what controls are placed on them?

Do you have an incident response plan for addressing the loss of your own or a customer's intellectual property?

## TIER TWO. *Core Security Infrastructure and Processes*

Do you allow anything in your network to talk directly to the internet?

Do you allow single-factor authentication for remote access?

How do you manage your internet gateways?

## TIER THREE. *Advanced Defenses*

How do you use and store network traffic?

Is there a central authority governing all of your active directory domains?

How do you get your actionable, unclassified cyber intelligence?

Do you employ a data-leak prevention product as part of an insider threat program?

# Assessing the Board's Cyber Risk
# Oversight Effectiveness

*Questions Directors Can Ask to Assess the Board's Cyber Literacy*

Can all directors effectively contribute to a robust conversation with management about the current state of the company's cybersecurity? In which areas does our lack of knowledge/ understanding of cyber matters prevent effective oversight?

Are we able to effectively interpret/assess management's presentations and their answers to our questions?

Do we thoroughly understand the most significant cyber threats to this business and what impacts they could have on the company's strategy and ultimately on its long-term growth?

Is the organization adequately monitoring current and potential cybersecurity-related legislation and regulation?

Does the company have insurance that covers cyber events, and what exactly is covered? Is there director and officer exposure if we don't carry adequate insurance? What are the benefits beyond risk transfer of carrying cyber-risk insurance?

Does our organization participate in any of the public- or private-sector ecosystem-wide cybersecurity and information-sharing organizations?

Is the organization adequately monitoring current and potential cybersecurity-related legislation and regulation?

Does the company have insurance that covers cyber events, and what exactly is covered? Is there director and officer exposure if we don't carry adequate insurance? What are the benefits beyond risk transfer of carrying cyber-risk insurance?

## The Cyber Insider Threat— a Real and Ever-Present Danger

Careless workers: employees or partners who non-maliciously misappropriate resources, break acceptable use policies, mishandle data, install unauthorized applications, or use unapproved workarounds

Inside agents: insiders recruited, solicited, or bribed by external parties to exfiltrate data

Disgruntled employees: insiders recruited, solicited, or bribed by external parties to exfiltrate data

Malicious insiders: actors with access to corporate assets who use existing privileges to access information for personal gain

Feckless third parties: business partners who compromise security through negligence, misuse, or malicious access to, or use of, an asset

This tool will help boards of directors ask senior management the right questions to ensure that these wide-ranging cyber insider threats are being properly mitigated.

## Questions Boards Should Ask Senior Management About Insider Threats

What systems are in place (background checks, channels that allow employees to report concerns, etc.) to vet employees and identify malicious behavior? Is there a strong collaboration between information security, physical security, general counsel, human resources, corporate investigations, and other key partners in managing these systems?

Do employees only gain access to the data and systems necessary to their jobs (no more, no less)? How is access managed when an employee leaves the company or accepts a new position within the company?

Does the security team know exactly which employees have elevated privileges, and are they monitored to ensure that they are not abusing their access?

Are processes and technologies in place to detect and prevent information from leaving the network? Are these enforced to control the use of removable media (like USB drives)?

Is a data classification policy in place and enforced to ensure proper labeling and handling?

Do we periodically test them with internal assets and external parties to validate their effectiveness?

Do we have a comprehensive incident response plan involving all stakeholders (human resources, the general counsel, compliance, security, others)? Is there a strong relationship with law enforcement partners for incident response? Are there in-house forensic capabilities, or is an outside firm on retainer?

Do we have a backup and recovery program? Could we recover our systems and critical data if access were prevented or data corrupted in the main system? Do we have strong controls around our critical vendor relationships?

## Supply-Chain and Third-Party Risks

*Questions Directors Can Ask to Assess the Company's*
*Approach to Cyber Supply-Chain Risk Management*

1. How do we balance the financial opportunities (lower costs, higher efficiency, etc.) created by greater supply-chain flexibility with potentially higher cyber risks? Here are some items to consider:

   a) Risk and reward analysis, and accounting for cyber-security management and information technology governance in the total cost of ownership calculation

   b) Negotiation strategies inclusive of cybersecurity insurance provisions

   c) Implementation of service-level agreements inclusive of reporting, metrics, and ongoing monitoring requirements

2. What do we need to do to fully include cybersecurity in current supply-chain risk management? Here are some items to consider:

   a) Training supply-chain personnel to recognize cyber-security risk and enabling mitigation activities

   b) Third-party due diligence throughout the proposal, selection, and onboarding processes

   c) Cybersecurity expertise leveraged during the negotiating and contracting process

3. How are cybersecurity requirements built into contracts and service-level agreements? How are they enforced? Contracts and service-level agreements can be written to include requirements for the following:

a) Cybersecurity insurance provisions

b) Personnel policies such as background checks, training, etc.

c) Access controls

d) Encryption, backup, and recovery policies

e) Secondary access to data

## Questions Boards Should Ask Senior Management on Incident Response

1. Is there an incident playbook with clear definitions of incidents, roles and responsibilities, and escalation processes? Are core business functions such as IT, business, legal, and communication integrated into the response plan? How does it fit into the company's overall crisis and business recovery plan?

2. What are the escalation criteria for notifying senior leadership and the board if necessary? Who has the final decision-making authority?

3. Is the organizational resiliency tested around large risk scenarios and exercised through tabletops and common threat simulation?

4. Are there established relationships with the intel community and key regulators? Have information-sharing relationships been established through information sharing and analysis centers and consortiums and with other companies?

5. Does the organization have notification and mandatory reporting obligations (e.g., in regard to regulations of the US Securities and Exchange Commission, the General Data Protection Regulation, the Department of Defense and its Defense Security Service for cleared contractors, and the federal government)?

What are they?

6. What are the criteria and what is the process for disclosing incidents to investors?

7. What can we do to mitigate the losses from an incident?

8. What are the critical, key performance indicators used to measure incident response effectiveness (e.g., time to detect and time to respond)?

9. What key steps do you follow after a critical incident? What steps do you follow to ensure this type of incident doesn't occur again?

   a) Requirements around the use of subcontractors

   b) Countries where data will be stored

   c) Data-security standards and notification requirements for data breaches or other cyber incidents

   d) Incident-response plans

   e) Audits of cybersecurity practices and/or regular certifications of compliance

   f) Participation in testing and contingency activities

Requirements for timely return/destruction of data at termination

1. Do our vendor agreements provide adequate controls for legal risks and compliance requirements (e.g., FTC, HIPAA, GDPR, etc.)? Here are some items to consider:

   a) Access to confidential or proprietary data, personally identifiable information (PII), sensitive personal information (SPI), or handling of personal health information

   b) Data used for regulatory, financial, or other internal reporting provided by a third party

    c) Third-party compliance with laws, regulations, policies, and regulatory guidance

2. Are we indemnified against security incidents on the part of our suppliers/vendors? Here are some items to consider:

    a) Breach, incidents, and vulnerabilities

    b) Limitation of liability

    c) Intellectual property violations

## SITUATIONAL AWARENESS

AT THE BATTLE of Gettysburg, the adversaries were slowly drawn into sending in the right soldiers and armaments, but they didn't realize that this skirmish was evolving into a titanic battle that would determine the outcome of the war.

Don't lose sight of the broader picture by busying yourself with only going down checklists. If you do, you might miss the underlying direction of the situation in front of you. Checklists are a component of cybersecurity, but you have to have an understanding of how a situation is evolving.

# chapter nine

# THE HOLOCAUST AND THE SEEDS OF DATA PRIVACY REGULATION

*Privacy means people know what they're signing up for, in plain language, and repeatedly. I believe people are smart. Some people want to share more than other people do. Ask them.*

—Steve Jobs, Apple co-founder (1955–2011)

D URING THE CORONAVIRUS PANDEMIC, DIVERGENT means of handling the outbreak were employed.

In China, the government effectively instituted martial law where a person could be arrested for not wearing a mask in public. They quarantined citizens and moved one-quarter of all of their doctors and nurses from around the country into one region. This was enforceable in part because, from a cultural perspective, China thinks of community first and individual second.

During the writing of this book, tragedies unfolded in Italy, Spain, and, eventually, the United States—countries where their ideologies put the individual first. As I wrote this chapter, we were in the early stages of the pandemic before the numbers of infections and deaths climbed at such an alarming rate. I walked around my city block and practiced social distancing, and I recognized that I was able to do that due in part to the fact that the West, and America in particular, appreciates the rights of an individual—perhaps to a fault in some circumstances.

This emphasis on the individual has significant implications when it comes to the world of data privacy.

We can debate when privacy first came into social consciousness. The early Christian practices of seclusion and the 1215 decision by the Fourth Council of Lateran that confession should be mandatory for the masses and kept private are just some examples.

Let's instead use the date the industry most recognizes as the point at which privacy was born.

In "The Right to Privacy," published on December 15, 1890, in the *Harvard Law Review,* Samuel D. Warren and Louis D. Brandeis stated:

> The intensity and complexity of life, attendant upon advancing civilization, have rendered necessary some retreat from the world, and man, under the refining influence of culture, has become more sensitive to publicity, so that solitude and privacy have become more essential to the individual; but modern enterprise and invention have, through invasions upon his privacy, subjected him to mental pain and distress, far greater than could be inflicted by mere bodily injury.

This concept of the rights of an individual has been building for more than one hundred years. The concept has gained momentum because some of the obstacles we, as people, have faced.

As the Nazis were coming to power in the 1930s, they gathered information on non-Aryans, specifically targeting Jewish and Polish citizens. As we now well know, they used this information to systematically remove the rights of those individuals. At first, people were no longer allowed to have a cat, then a dog. Later, others weren't allowed to shop in certain stores. Then they were only allowed to live in a certain section of the city. Gradually, the Germans—specifically non-ethnic Germans—had their rights taken away.

The end result was the horror of the Holocaust.

Having learned from the tragedy and all that led up to it, the European Union (EU) has since been a leader in and champion of individual data privacy rights. Most recently, they built upon this stance with the release of the General Data Protection Regulation (GDPR) in May of 2018, which was a significant step in extending a person's privacy rights.

If you're a company anywhere in the world and you gather information on a European citizen, whether you do business in Europe or not, you are subject to the regulation and its associated fines. The regulation actually forces companies to raise their game when it comes to data hygiene. To comply, companies must improve their understanding of the data they collect, what they store, what they process, how they protect it, and how they enforce the right to be forgotten.

If an EU citizen wants to have their data removed because they no longer have a relationship with a business, they can send a request, and the organization is obligated to find that person's data and delete it permanently. That right to be forgotten was a powerful control that's difficult to implement, and it cost companies all over the world hundreds of millions to billions of dollars to comply.

Much like security talent, experienced privacy professionals are a rare commodity. They need to have a somewhat hybrid background. They must understand compliance and the legalese of it and also have a basic understanding of safety, security, and data privacy. Organizations such as the International Association of Privacy Professionals now offer various certifications to help the industry implement this regulation.

The EU's view of privacy regulation is being adopted more broadly in the US. Each state has a different data privacy notification law. California has been at the vanguard of data privacy protection for years, passing the California Consumer Protection Act (CCPA). The act is quite similar to the GDPR and raises the stakes for California-based companies and organizations.

Privacy practitioners will say that security professionals are tone-deaf and color-blind to privacy nuances and that security and privacy are paradoxical—that you can't have privacy without security. Your privacy or your identifiable information needs to be protected in some form or fashion.

But if you have too much security—if you're doing too much monitoring, if you're collecting data and then using it for a different purpose—then you're actually *violating* an individual's data privacy.

We came to our jobs from different backgrounds and with different skillsets. As such, it took me a number of years working on privacy projects to develop a perspective and appreciation for what this attorney was saying.

If, for example, I collect your name, social security number, date of birth, and credit information as part of your mortgage application, I have an obligation to protect that information as per various laws, rules, and regulations. I also cannot analyze that data and take the fact that you might have a strong credit rating and sell that information to an independent third-party. If I do, that party now has your information and will use it to sell you something that increases their revenue.

That is the security and privacy paradox. You need to protect the data you collect and use it only for the intention for which you collected it. Using it for secondary and tertiary purposes that might benefit you in some form would be highly unethical and leads down a very slippery slope.

## Critical Security Controls 13 and 14: Data Protection[21] and Controlled Access Based on the Need to Know[22]

Granting the right access to the right resources to the right people is critical.

In many ways, the notion of identity and access management has become the new frontier of digital defense and cybersecurity. There was a time when we had multiple layers of defense, but now with the mobility of data and the existence of the cloud, we are faced with how to protect our identities as we navigate the digital world.

CSC 13 relates to the idea that overly permissive access controls can breach privacy rights. Your company must consider how you manage access at a number of endpoints.

How do your employees enter your building? Is it via badge swipe or with video recognition?

It is critical that you continue to tighten the access control as someone approaches a greater and greater value at risk. It's easy to walk into a bank and withdraw cash. It's far more difficult to walk into Fort Knox and do the same. While those are two extremes, they are an example of how to think about the data in your organization.

As data's value increases, so should data protection. Develop processes and tools to prevent data exfiltration and to mitigate the effects of exfiltration, particularly when that data is personal information that can be used to harm a person.

---

[21] "CIS Control 3: Data Recovery Capability," Center for Internet Security, accessed May 18, 2021, https://www.cisecurity.org/controls/data-protection/.

[22] "The 18 CIS Controls," Center for Internet Security, accessed May 18, 2021, https://www.cisecurity.org/controls/controlled-access-based-on-the-need-to-know/.

As relates to CSC 14, you must control data on a need-to-know basis.

If you're a small company that's just getting started, most of your employees will have access to most information. As you grow, accumulate financials, and have to become compliant with Sarbanes-Oxley, controlled access based on need-to-know becomes critical. Your employees should only have access to the systems, applications, and data they need to get their jobs done and nothing more.

This is the concept of role-based access control. An accountant can have access to a system regarding financial reporting, but they cannot have access to your human resources information.

The Fair Information Practice Principles[23] (FIPPs) came from the Federal Trade Commission (FTC) as best practices for managing the digital rights of citizens. The principles provide a framework around what private information is being collected, stored, processed, and transmitted. The FIPPs provide transparency into how that information will be put to use by an organization requesting it, as well as how an individual can request access to their information and the steps that a company will take to make it confidential.

It is incumbent upon you to adopt this framework as it relates to the private information of both your employees and consumers.

## KNOWLEDGE-BASED AUTHENTICATION

BECAUSE OF THE advent of the internet of things, there are items in organizations the world over that listen to us. These items were placed there intentionally by us.

---

[23] "ResourceCenter," iapp, accessed May 18, 2021, https://iapp.org/resources/article/fair-information-practices/.

The trouble is, if you don't update the software on those devices, a hacker can compromise them. If the end-user company doesn't implement the right data protection controls, then they have the right to collect that data and use it to cross-sell you. Worse yet, they could potentially lose that data, and it could be used against you.

Social media killed what was known as knowledge-based authentication. An example of knowledge-based authentication was when an individual called into a bank and the staff asked that person for their mother's maiden name, date of birth, and favorite color for validation. Now that same information is readily available via our social media accounts, which nullified an entire method of security and control.

If Moore's law was that computing power is going to double every eighteen months or so, then one might argue that there's a Zuckerberg's law—that we're more than likely to share twice as much information about ourselves every eighteen months or so.

Before the advent of Facebook, would you have shared any of the information you do today broadly, to anyone who can see it? Of course, you can take some safeguards and precautions and only allow your friends access to this information. But we know that Google, Facebook, and many other companies deal not just with thousands but *millions* of compromised accounts *every day*.

That means all of the information you think is protected is potentially up for grabs. Some of the more sophisticated attacks will leverage trust-based relationships—such as a friend on Facebook—and will send you something that has a payload that drops malware onto your machine.

We began this chapter talking about privacy and the right to privacy—or lack thereof—in World War II Germany. This concept of digital privacy ties into trust.

> ➤ Whom do you trust?
> ➤ Why do you trust them?
> ➤ How do you validate that trust?
> ➤ Will they use the information about you for good or for ill?

Unfortunately, in many cases, that trust is being broken and exploited for some sort of nefarious gain. It's so important to defend an individual's right to privacy because misuse of information and violation of trust are a slippery slope. Today it might cost you financially —but will it be used against your human rights tomorrow? I realize my early experiences in the Soviet Union color my perspective, but, once again, only the paranoid will survive.

Identity is the perimeter, and we used to have more well-defined perimeters.

Whether you were a domestic company or a global one, the perimeter was your firewall, the barricade around your castle. With the advent of cloud-based technology, you started to migrate your data outside of that firewall into someone else's castle. Then, with mobile technology, you began to allow people to traverse those castle walls.

So, while defense and depth still apply to a number of our organizations today, the cloud and mobile arrivals and all the benefits that ensue have also created a problem, one where the perimeter is no longer the firewall—it's the identity of the individual.

Identity is the new frontier in security and privacy. When you join a company, they create an identity for you. In larger businesses, that identity will follow you as you move through the organization. There is an entire space in technology called identity and access management that handles your identity through a digital environment when you join, move throughout, and/or leave the company.

## LEVERAGE THE DISCIPLINE

IF YOU'RE A chief financial officer, you know that you need to understand your financial inflows and outflows.

You need to track your financial data based on generally accepted accounting principles and to understand the sources of data. If you're publishing financials, you need to be adherent to Sarbanes-Oxley, or SOX. That requires gathering data from across your organization and making sure that good hygiene was applied to those numbers. Then you need to publish it in a 10-K or other financial report for the CEO to sign off on.

These widely accepted accounting principles are very similar to the principles you should apply to data privacy.

Instead of numbers, in data privacy you deal with names and people. The same discipline and level of effort that organizations have spent gathering financial numbers for well over a century must now be applied to how you handle data. The same type of discipline and assigning of stewards and curators also applies. There must be ways of identifying where the sources of information are, where they're coming from, and what the associated risks are.

Recall that there is approximately $200 of risk associated with every record of an individual you have. That's why insurance companies now offer data privacy and cybersecurity insurance. Does that apply in a linear fashion? Meaning, if you've got a million records, do you have $202 million of risk?

Likely not, as there are diminishing losses associated, but understanding that risk curve and your risk tolerance for having a privacy data breach and the fines associated with it is critical. Companies used to adopt the attitude that they would just pay for credit monitoring and privacy notice breaches, but the EU General Data Protection Regulation changed that, as the GDPR can take a portion of up to 4 percent of your global revenue if you don't handle their regulated information correctly. This potentially leaves you with hundreds of millions of dollars in fines.

Leverage the discipline that you have developed in your own financial monitoring and reporting and apply that mindset to developing a privacy program with similarly dedicated personnel, technologies, and outcomes.

Because the reality of the situation is that sometimes the industry gets ahead of regulations and then the regulations try to catch up, resulting in a whipsaw effect. Many of the digital giants ran ahead and used our private information in order to grow their organizations, and now the regulations are trying to adapt. There is now this unevenness of a new regulatory burden.

In order to be an enlightened organization in the twenty-first century digital age, you must have good data usage practices, but many companies—perhaps including yours—are stuck. They haven't invested in this space. The good news is there's no time like the present to start. Whether or not you employ specific data privacy professionals, you can leverage people with that mindset. This typically includes those who have worked in compliance or who have a regulatory understanding —perhaps someone in finance or legal.

Big things have small beginnings. Start by leveraging your existing investments that already have a control-oriented mindset to begin building your privacy program.

That's a step in the right direction.

chapter ten

# THE INVASION OF NORMANDY AND SURVIVOR BIAS

*Gentlemen, we have run out of money;*
*now we have to think.*

—Winston Churchill (1874–1965)

J UNE 6, 1944. WORLD WAR II, D-DAY.

As part of Operation Fortitude South, the Allies attempted to fool the Nazis by creating a fake army under General Patton to make them think an invasion was imminent from southeast England. While they did this, the Allies subsequently launched an attack under General Eisenhower.

So, as the boats were landing on the beaches, the Allies sent B-17 planes to carpet bomb Normandy. These planes had a high mortality rate—they were shot out of the sky at a much higher frequency than the Allies had expected. As the B-17s landed in the English airfields, the United States Army Air Corps (USAAC) analyzed the damage (there was no Air Force at the time).

They noticed that a disproportionate number of the returning planes had the nose blown off. Their initial reaction to this finding was to take precautionary measures to harden the nose of the plane. They went about the business of doing so on both new and existing planes.

Then a mathematician named Abraham Wald performed another analysis and discovered that the nose of the plane was *not* the weak area that needed to be hardened.

Due to survivor bias, the USAAC was only sampling a subset of the total population—in this case, the survivors of the battles that returned. In doing so, they made an error in their decision-making process about where to harden the plane.

Wald stated that if the USAAC were to measure the full population of planes that were flying into battle, they would notice that the untouched portions of the planes that were returning were actually the weakest and most fragile. In other words, planes that *were* hit over Normandy in that untouched section of the plane were going down. The planes that sustained damage to the nose were still able to fly and eventually return to base where they could be repaired.

## SURVIVOR BIAS AND CYBERSECURITY

COMPANIES AND BUSINESSES, in particular, are experiencing some form of cyberattack taking place at any given location and at any given time. When there is a breach—a malicious software breach, for example—companies can experience a negative outcome in a variety of ways.

Organizations today (and for several years now) have been targeted by what are known as ransomware attacks. In these instances, an attacker targets the victim using a trusted email source or website. These attackers purchase advertisements on sites that you know and trust, and when you click on said advertisement, it downloads malicious software onto your computer. From there, it will redirect itself to another site to pull down a separate payload of data, and then that software will build itself up on your endpoint in a program that will commit some sort of malicious action.

These can include stealing your credentials as you type, stealing your information, or—in the case of ransomware—it will encrypt your laptop or desktop and write itself on any resources to which you have access. For example, if you were to go to a popular website and click on a malicious ad, your laptop would get locked up, and the malware would write itself to any file shares that you can access. Many organizations have had numerous resources locked up for ransom by these types of attacks.

When this happens, you are then compelled to pay the attacker, most often in cryptocurrency because it is untraceable in most cases. You'll also have to do this within a certain time frame. If you don't pay, you'll lose those resources if you haven't backed them up.

This is a *multimillion-dollar* business for these attackers.

Organizations typically respond to the population that was impacted by the attack. Unfortunately, they don't take into consideration the broader environment in regard to which controls worked to prevent the attack and which ones didn't.

Imagine a company attacked by malware that infests a number of machines. Of course, that company will look at those infected machines in particular. In doing so, they will be blind to the subset of laptops and desktops that were not impacted.

If, however, they are aware of their survivor bias and pause to ask themselves why some assets were affected by the malware while others were not, they can dig deeper and find that the malware may have been so sophisticated that it was operating-system aware.

An operating-system-aware malware lands on your laptop and performs a quick scan of the environment. It specifically checks the registry, and if it spots a characteristic in the operating system that is typical of malware analyzers, it will go dormant.

In other words, if a malware finds itself landing on a cryptocurrency researcher's laptop, thinking that it was in a sandbox environment being monitored so someone could develop an antivirus for it, it will turn itself off.

In our example, the sophistication of the malware tells the company something. The organization sampled a broader population—just as Wald did with the B-17 bombers—and discovered that the malware had this attribute of what appeared to be a string to check what type of operating systems it was executing on.

And what did *that* tell them?

Since that malware was looking for certain characteristics to make it go dormant, the organization will replicate those registry characteristics on their endpoints. Doing so will inoculate themselves to that particular type of malware. This makes those endpoints appear to be security research boxes and protects them from that threat.

Using Wald's mental model, you can approach a malware outbreak using behavioral analysis and a broadening of your sample environment to create your own immunization to the threats you face.

## Critical Security Controls 8, 19, and 20: Malware Defenses,[24] Incident Response and Management,[25] and Penetration Tests and Red Team Exercises[26]

Most malware is sent via phishing. An attacker pretends to be someone else, they send you a link to an executable file, and you click on that link and download malicious software to your endpoint.

That software might take the form of ransomware or a Trojan designed to monitor keystrokes. The more sophisticated attacks will lead you to click a link that takes you to a website where they'll partially download an encrypted piece of malware that you can't inspect. Then they'll redirect you to another site where you'll download the second part of the payload, which will build itself up like a LEGO set and infect your machine.

Antivirus programs have been on endpoints for well over twenty years and, by all means, organizations should invest in them—but you must also update your malware defenses.

There is a new malware released *every day*, with millions and millions of variants. You must have detection in place that does regular scans, files integrity monitoring, and checks on your web reputation. That last piece is critical because many attackers today are creating fake sites to replicate a business so that users will

---

[24] "CIS Control 10: Malware Defenses," Center for Internet Security, accessed May 18, 2021, https://www.cisecurity.org/controls/malware-defenses/.

[25] "CIS Control 17: Incident Response and Management," Center for Internet Security, accessed May 18, 2021, https://www.cisecurity.org/controls/incident-response-and-management/.

[26] "The 18 CIS Controls," Center for Internet Security, accessed May 18, 2021, https://www.cisecurity.org/controls/penetration-tests-and-red-team-exercises/.

download malicious software from them. This puts your employees and clients at risk.

In keeping with the lesson regarding survivor bias, your incident response and management and the process of your penetration testing should not just look at the assets that have been impacted. You must also examine the broader population of endpoints to understand the scope of the attack—to understand what defenses worked and which ones didn't. Doing this also helps you understand and assess the resilience of your business and network when bad things happen.

When thinking about these three CSCs in the frame of survivor bias, consider the Decision Matrix,[27] based on the Eisenhower Matrix.

Dwight Eisenhower once said that in terms of prioritization, that which is important is rarely urgent, and that which is urgent is rarely important. This notion helped him think through challenges in a simple way. The Decision Matrix breaks down challenges to allow you to prioritize, as well as to make long-term decisions.

Awareness of survivor bias should factor into your long-term plan. Ask yourself how you are going to make investments in your digital security that are consequential and irreversible. You should also realize that those investments should be made more thoughtfully than those that can be reversible and are inconsequential.

The Decision Matrix is a tool that business leaders and those who are responsible for managing technology risk can leverage as they think through how they respond to issues. They can do this while keeping their true north on their radar, making meaningful decisions for long-term improvements.

---

[27] "The Decision Matrix: How to Prioritize What Matters," *Farnam Street*, accessed February 12, 2021, https://fs.blog/2018/09/decision-matrix/.

## CORKSCREW THINKING

WHEN THE BRITISH were outnumbered and outgunned by the Nazis in the dark days of World War II, Winston Churchill brought together a group of leaders and told them they'd run out of time and money. Now they would have to think through their problems.

In doing so, he applied what he called corkscrew thinking.

### How Do You Exit the Maze?

Take a look at the image below and find a way from start to finish in your mind's eye.

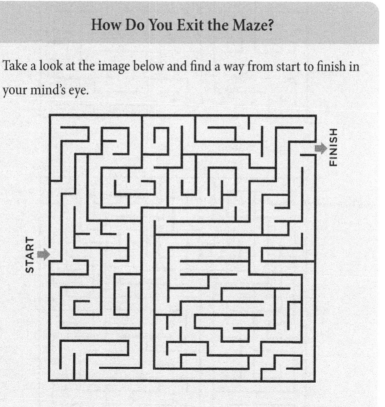

This is the path most people choose.

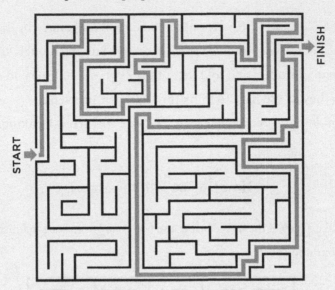

Anyone think of doing this?

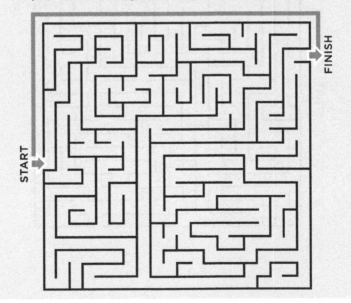

What are the rules? Why do they exist? Are these truly two-dimensional mazes or can we just do this?

**Disruptive thinking makes new rules or a new system.
What assumptions are impeding your speed right now?**

Assumptions impede our corkscrew thinking.

Even with the loosest of parameters, many would go through the maze, start to finish, doing their best to avoid all the blockades in front of them.

However, it's possible to get to the other side by completely circumventing those walls in front of you — *if,* when thinking about challenges you've never seen before, you pay attention to your own biases and self-induced limitations.

Then and only then can you devise a way to the other side that avoids those obstacles.

Churchill asked this question: how do we trick the Germans into believing something that would benefit the British Army and the British effort? The answer was especially important because the Germans were running counterintelligence and were already very wary about the British intelligence they were intercepting.

Corkscrew thinking is akin to out-of-the-box thinking, and it relates to a survivor being survivor-bias aware. It is in your toolkit of mental models that you can apply when dealing with situations that you've not seen before, which is especially useful in twenty-first-century digital risk management.

In many cases, organizations practice good hygiene, utilize best practices, and apply the top twenty security controls. In several other cases, however, issues come up that are completely foreign, and for which there is no playbook. This is where corkscrew thinking comes in, thinking through problems using tactics such as root cause analysis and the Lean Six Sigma Five Whys.

When you think through what an attacker is trying to do, you have to consider what they want and what tools are at their disposal to get it. You must determine their balconies (their strengths) and their basements (their weaknesses).

Churchill did this throughout World War II, and he used this way of thinking to plant information. For example, he had information for battle plans placed on a dead body that washed up ashore. The Nazis found it, believed it, and through the various steps that Churchill and his intelligence team had taken, fell into the trap the British had designed.

Corkscrew thinking means thinking through the various dimensions, permutations, and probabilities of problems you're facing. Part of that means eliminating your survivor-bias, broadening your field of view, and considering different angles when it comes to protecting your digital assets.

When you do this, you'll realize the same results the Allies did when they took Abraham Wald's analysis into account. Once the USAAC assessed and hardened the truly weak points of the B-17 bombers, their mortality rate dropped significantly.

Similarly, when our imaginary company applied the registry characteristic to their network endpoints, they immunized themselves to the malware, taking the perceived strength of its operating system awareness and turning it into a weakness.

It's worth noting, however, that you don't want to be quite as tactical as our unnamed but real-world company in the case of the malware threat.

That organization was reacting to a "fire alarm" on an attack that had circumvented multiple layers of their control. In this particular case, making a change on the endpoints' registry didn't foundationally change their risk profile. It inoculated them to a temporary threat and bought them time to enhance their controls in other areas. This thereby reduced the probability of future malware attacks. They strengthened their email gateway and how they interrogated those emails, as well as strengthened their proxy servers and the sort of data they were allowed to pull.

While this was effective, you need to balance discipline and rigor with creative improvisation—the daily work you do is disciplined and rigorous, but sometimes life throws you a curveball, a risk to your security different than any other you've seen before. That's where improvisation comes into play. It's about having the ability to think through problems critically using mental models and the like to solve an issue previously undealt with.

Want to learn more about corkscrew thinking?

The first step in this journey is developing the unquestionable thirst to read and learn from others. Read on topics outside of your expertise. Read on the hard sciences that allow for falsifiability, such as physics, chemistry, biology, astronomy, geology, and meteorology. Reading up on historical figures, events, trends, and cultures can tie into the journey to attain a sort of polymath status that includes a wide range of knowledge. Not coincidentally, Winston Churchill was one of history's great polymaths.

Falsifiability or refutability is the capacity for a theory, hypothesis, or statement to be contradicted by evidence or proved wrong. First introduced by Karl Popper (1902–1994) in his book *The Logic of Scientific Discovery*, understanding these concepts will help you think through the soft sciences.

The soft sciences of psychology, sociology, anthropology, and, in some ways, archaeology, have variables more difficult to isolate and predict—but knowledge and appreciation of the interplay will enrich your perspective.

## THE FULL PICTURE

ALWAYS ASK YOURSELF if you're looking at the full picture relevant to the decisions that you need to make or if you're looking at a subsection of the picture. Then ask yourself if you're making decisions on that subsection that impact the whole picture.

If your network has been compromised by malware, do you only look at the portion that's been compromised, or do you factor in the elements that have not? As with the Battle of Normandy, when you step back from the situation and sample the entire ecosystem, you can see why certain things go right *and* why certain things go wrong.

A software solution that helps companies manage their IP addresses found itself in the news in 2020. The solution was a fairly benign piece of network management software. Malicious attackers broke into the company, infiltrated its software development, and planted malware. That malware was then certified by the company, legitimizing the software. They then pushed it out to all of their clients.

These clients ran those infected versions of the software, and those infected versions performed a DNS lookup for the bad actors, allowing them to look at the source of highly sensitive IP addresses, including those of government organizations. These attackers then established connections with those networks and sent a DNS kill command that created a huge supply-chain and risk-management issue.

But the industry found itself trying to understand the full picture of the breach because they only knew about a subset of the companies and no one really knows how far the attackers went into those companies or what they stole.

In order to know those things, the industry would have to step back and look at *all* of the companies impacted—including those that weren't obviously affected. Only then can they understand how the attackers were able to successfully compromise them.

Don't only study the B-17 bombers coming home—consider the ones that didn't come back.

chapter eleven

# PLANNING FALLACY AND THE SYDNEY OPERA HOUSE

*A goal without a plan*
*is just a wish.*

—Antoine de Saint-Exupery (1900–1944)

W HEN THE POWERS THAT BE IN THE AUSTRALIAN
government decided to build the Sydney Opera House,
they knew they wanted to make a statement on the world
stage.

They put out bids to design it and architects from all over made
a slew of proposals. It seemed a good problem to have. But they ran
into another one—of their own making.

The winning proposal, while avant-garde, modern, and futuris-
tic-looking, was not well vetted. It answered the question, "What are
you going to do?" But no one stopped to ask, "How are you going to
do it?"

And they should have—because the architect had no idea how he
was going to build his own design.

In fact, the tools and expertise to build what he was proposing
didn't even exist. When the government accepted the proposal, they
had no inkling how long the journey was going to take and how much
it was going to cost.

This scenario plays itself out in organizations frequently.

When we think about our risk appetite or risk tolerance, we think
about how much we are willing to lose and what risk we're willing to
accept. Almost across the board, organizations tend to place the most
weight on software development projects, and invariably we see these
big, large-scale, multiyear, multimillion-dollar projects fail.

And they don't just fail. They struggle to be on time, on budget, and to address the requirements that were initially set.

There's a body of research that suggests for every project that creates software in an organization, there is a 1.2 percent chance that software will be written off. This means that the project fails and the company writes it off their books at 1.2 percent every month that it goes on. The longer the project lasts—say a yearlong monolithic software implementation—whether it's for security, or really any other product, there is an increased chance (approximately 14 percent) that you're going to write it off. And it compounds over the course of time.

Organizations are moving away from traditional waterfall methodology—the multiyear, multimillion-dollar, monolithic approach—especially when it comes to legacy software. Now companies tend more toward Agile or modern delivery, which involves a multidisciplinary team of subject matter experts coming together and working in sprints to deliver incremental benefits. They bring together the correct subject matter expertise at the right time, using the right tools.

Agile development came out of Google in the early 2000s. Yes, it is more broadly adopted by cloud-native organizations and companies that started themselves in the cloud. It's widely seen as the modern delivery approach of the future.

To be fair, though, Agile doesn't work for everything. It's effective for new products based in the cloud for incremental improvements, but it would not be a fit for managing legacy mainframe systems.

That is why it's critical for an organization to have employees with subject matter expertise and critical thinking skills who can understand, based on what's worked in the past, what will work in the future. But one size does not fit all. It's about knowing when to apply the right tools at the right time.

Agile is a hot topic today in digital transformations and is referred to as DevSecOps, short for development, security, and operations. The goal is to make everyone accountable for security with the objective of implementing security decisions and actions at the same scale and speed as development and operations decisions and actions.

It's the concept of shift-left, getting security by design, and skin in the game.

In many cases, companies are making the same mistake as the planning fallacy of the Sydney Opera House. They decide they want to build a particular piece of software and agree to move forward, putting in place a budget, the people, and any other resources necessary.

Then, once the company begins building, they realize they don't have the tools or subject matter expertise, and that the project is going to cost far more than they had expected. The question then becomes: how can they leverage modern delivery in order to reduce those probabilities? In other words, how can they validate that they have the right expertise and the right tools and build the software in bite-sized chunks?

The modern delivery approach of Agile software delivery lets you eat the elephant one bite at a time.

But how do you weave in security to this methodology?

You do it at the onset of the project—security by design, risk management by design. Even if you don't have a security expert on your team working on software delivery in Agile, you have security champions who are aware enough to "phone home" and get the right guidance and expertise. This will ensure that protections are being built into your software development lifecycle as you're building the new pieces and complying with laws, rules, and regulations.

These champions will adhere to good development practices as espoused by organizations like the Open Web Application Security Project (OWASP). They won't introduce seeds of risk at the onset. OWASP is an online community that produces freely available articles, methodologies, documentation, tools, and technologies in the field of web application security. The technical specifics listed in OWASP can then be adopted at the earliest onset of product and technology development in the shift-left concept where these concerns are addressed at the conception.

At this point, you might ask: why doesn't everyone do this?

I'd respond by asking why people continue to smoke when they know it will kill them?

It's human behavior.

Balancing disciplined structure while enabling creative improvisation can help navigate uncharted waters.

Using RACI can help. RACI is an acronym for responsible, accountable, consulted, and informed. It is a matrix of activities and decision-making tied to team, roles, and/or people. In this case, we will call the person the resource.

The definitions of the RACI categories are:

> Responsible: resource performing an activity or does the work
> Accountable: resource ultimately accountable and has yes/no/ veto power
> Consulted: resource contributing feedback to the activity
> Informed: resource needing to know of the decision or action

Accountability is key. As Charlie Munger said, "Show me the incentive and I will show you the outcome." It's the chicken and the pig from Chapter One—who is all in, shifting left, and getting security by design at the developer level? Accountability drives commitment. Be 100 percent satisfied with 100 percent commitment from your team, and be 100 percent dissatisfied with anything less.

RACIs help in workload analysis, work assignments, project management, and broad efforts that span business units. If organizations are naturally beginning to self-silo, RACIs are a great tool to build bridges across those divisions and belong in your toolbox along with OKRs and the other tool sets we've covered.

## Critical Security Controls 10, 15, and 18: Data Recovery Capabilities,[28] Wireless Access Control on the Need to Know,[29] and Application Software Security[30]

Every company wants to be resilient. In the case of an attack, they want to be able to recover.

It's possible you or your company has invested in legacy backups or systems that back up to the cloud—but how often are you testing them? How often are you restoring and validating that you

---

[28] "CIS Control 10: Malware Defenses," Center for Internet Security, accessed May 18, 2021, https://www.cisecurity.org/controls/data-recovery-capability/.

[29] "CIS Control 15: Service Provider Management," Center for Internet Security, accessed May 18, 2021, https://www.cisecurity.org/controls/wireless-access-control/.

[30] "CIS Control 16: Application Software Security," Center for Internet Security, accessed May 18, 2021, https://www.cisecurity.org/controls/application-software-security/.

can *actually* recover from an outage, interruption, or even a malicious attack?

It is essential to have a disciplined data recovery process in place so that your data is backed up every night to a trusted source from which you can restore your information. Investing in those capabilities is especially critical for companies that are becoming cloud-based. Even more importantly, you must ensure via periodic testing that your cloud service provider is able to recover your data should it be lost.

The addition of Wi-Fi within companies presented new opportunities, but it also meant that new tools had to be built to control the access. Those processes and tools used to track control and prevent assets that don't belong on your Wi-Fi from being there are a must. Without them, intruders can hop on your Wi-Fi and access your systems and records.

This should go without saying, but it is critical that your organization's Wi-Fi has complex passwords and that your encryption is set to the highest possible levels. You must also scan the assets on your network. If you're a company of one thousand employees, you will likely have much more than one thousand assets. The last thing you need is a large number of hangers-on taxing your resources and accessing your network. Wi-Fi management is key to protecting your network.

We are constantly injecting new software into our environments. As the architects of the Sydney Opera House were producing new construction methods and new tools, so too must you have a method in place to test the validity and integrity of the applications you introduce into your environment. Some of the more popular coding languages are fraught with security vulnerabilities. As organizations develop, they need to have a mature change-management process as to what they are letting into their network.

Additionally, as your company engages in software development and writes code, be sure that not only are the coders doing the writing and analyzing but that the security is looking for vulnerabilities that might be associated with that code. All involved must be sure the right configurations are being used and patches are applied as needed to prevent the risk exceptions that are the root cause of so many of the big breaches that make global news.

Much of this comes down to second-order thinking.

First-order thinking is the process of considering the intended and perhaps obvious implications of a business decision or policy change. Second-order thinking is the process of tracking down and then rallying the implications of those decisions or changes to potentially identify toxic combinations of features and functionality.

With the Sydney Opera House, the designers thought the structure would be beautiful and unique—but they didn't consider the implications of building something that had not been built before or the fact that they didn't have the tools to pull it off. They didn't apply second-order thinking.

This applies to your organization's risk management. If you make a decision to trust a new business partner and their software, second-order thinking will lead you to question what happens if that partner and their software are compromised. How would that affect *your* company? How could it cause *your* data to be compromised?

As the dot-com era began to take off and the launch of the Netscape browser made the internet more business-friendly, the very technology empowering businesses was also imperiling them through insecure web-browser transmissions. Cryptographer Taher Elgamal, Netscape's chief scientist at the time, became the driving force behind Secure Sockets Layer (SSL). SSL is the cryptographic protocol that provides communications security and trust in the digital age. Thinking beyond the immediate enabling of web-based transactions and creating a secure protocol helped accelerate the adoption of e-commerce.

Second-order thinking should be applied system-wide. No organization is an island. We depend on vendors as part of our supply chain. But we need to think about how our partners and supply chain, upstream or down, can impact us.

Ray Dalio once said:

"Failing to consider second- and third-order consequences is the cause of a lot of painfully bad decisions, and it is especially deadly when the first inferior option confirms your own biases. Don't seize on the first available option, no matter how good it seems, before you've asked questions and explored."[31]

Sound advice.

## PREMEDITATIO MALORUM

THE STOICS USED a technique called *premediatio malorum,* or premeditation of evils, to envision what negative outcomes can come in life. This practice is founded upon the belief that by imagining the worst-case scenario in advance, a practitioner is better prepared to prevent negative outcomes. It also better prepares them to manage failure when it occurs.

In premortem exercises, this is a valuable tool for laying out possibilities that you don't want to occur. Today we call this technique inversion.

---

[31] "Second-Order Thinking: What Smart People Use to Outperform." *Farnam Street,* accessed April 3, 2020, https://fs.blog/2016/04/second-order-thinking/.

Carl Jacobi, a German mathematician, was known for his ability to solve hard problems. His mantra was "invert, always invert." This approach helped him identify blind spots and errors missed at first glance.

Thinking ahead to potential undesirable outcomes, how your organization might arrive there, and working your way backward will create insights for your business and a more well-thought-out path forward.

Perhaps it's time to assign leaders in organizations specifically tasked with challenging groupthink and assumptions that could lead to blind spots and hazards. Perhaps it's time to embrace the role of a "chief dissent officer."

## PRE-MORTEMS

BUSINESS CONTINUITY/DISASTER RECOVERY exercises are key to organizational resilience. They test what a company would do should an interruption occur, ranging from human error to something more sinister, such as a DDoS attack. A DDoS is typically associated with some form of extortion, but in the world of normally distributed bell curves, the more likely causes are power outages or vendor issues.

Whether through qualitative experts' assertions or more quantitatively oriented Monte Carlo simulations, it is prudent to forecast what scenarios can interrupt your business. One or both can be used, but at the very least, in the continued spirit of know thyself, ask:

*Where are you sensitive to interruptions? Where are you fragile and susceptible to negative outcomes to your business?*

Disaster recovery (DR) drills fail a system or an application from one data center, and then fail it over to another. These span the geography of the network, taking highly critical systems, running them in one state, then failing them to run out of another state. These are fraught with bugs and gotchas and unknown-unknowns that pop up, along with known-unknowns, which make it hard to get a clean DR.

In 2007, Gary Klein (who continues to write about factors in human dynamics and behavior in planning) wrote "Performing a Project Premortem"[32] in the *Harvard Business Review*. The opening statement reads:

> **Projects fail at a spectacular rate. One reason is that too many people are reluctant to speak up about their reservations during the all-important planning phase. By making it safe for dissenters who are knowledgeable about the undertaking and worried about its weaknesses to speak up, you can improve a project's chances of success.**

Most people have heard of a postmortem, which is conducted when a project is complete, and everyone gets together to talk about what worked and what didn't. Human behavior comes into play because if you're sitting in a room and discussing what worked and didn't work with your boss present, and something you decided to do contributed to an issue that impacted the project, you might not be incentivized to call out that issue. As such, postmortems, while effective, don't tease out all of the potential issues of a project, product, or effort within an organization.

---

[32] Gary Klein, "Performing a Project Premortem," *Harvard Business Review*, accessed August 1, 2014, https://hbr.org/2007/09/performing-a-project-premortem.

A pre-mortem changes that dynamic.

In a pre-mortem, you gather the stakeholders and ask them to project into the future. A year from now, how might this project have failed?

For disaster recovery exercises, collect the best collective gotchas, particularly if they're ones you hadn't considered, and reward the individual who comes up with the best one with an expensive bottle of wine.

As you start on your project plan for a DR or software implementation, use this same pre-mortem scenario. Say a year or two has passed and the project is complete but didn't meet its objectives or was a total failure. How did it fail?

You'll see a completely different dynamic in these pre-mortems. Creative juices get flowing. People will call out issues much more readily, and those issues can be factored and implemented into your project. In the case of my company's DR exercises, our effectiveness went up using pre-mortems, meaning that recovery time was far shorter.

Leveraging that ability to forecast allows you to see around corners and lets you know whether or not that opera house can actually be built. It's like determining where the thin ice on the lake is. As we have discussed, like thin ice, vulnerabilities and weaknesses in your technology stack can land you in hot water if unseen and unremedied.

Pre-mortems also create a safe space, which can be an incredible morale booster for your team. Everyone wants to have a sense of purpose and meaning in their life, and they want to have a safe place to try and fail at their endeavors, as long as they can learn from them.

Pre-mortems allow the team to learn and grow together, which is fundamental to building morale. It allows people to bring the best, most authentic version of themselves to the workplace, which makes them want to be at work and deliver while they're there. When people are incentivized to call out issues, an organization's risk profile can be significantly reduced.

Getting creative, we can build on this concept and continue to incentivize participants to raise their hand and call out blind spots, surprises, and reality in general. If people see a process, system, or application that is unloved, poorly thought out, or that introduces risk to the organization, they call it out. An independent group of their peers will vet it, and if they've found a genuine issue, just as with the aforementioned bug bounties, they are publicly acknowledged with a physical award and cash prize, because no one says thank you like Benjamin Franklin.

Your project planning and the security of your company as a whole will be stronger when your team is engaged in this way. You want your people to come to work with a critical-thinking mindset and to create an environment in which they can raise their hand and have a voice. Not everyone needs or wants to be a leader, but everyone wants to feel they are heard and understood.

## CONTROL GATES

WHAT DOES THE Sydney Opera House tell us in terms of software design capabilities?

If you storyboard the creation of a piece of software, ask yourself: Do you have the tools? Do you have the assembly line secured? Are the right control gates in place so that you can actually deliver on your promise with *existing* tools, or do you need to invent or develop new ones?

# chapter twelve

# THE SPACE SHUTTLE AND THE NORMALIZATION OF RISK DEVIANCE

*Everyone thinks of changing the world, but no one thinks of changing himself.*

—Leo Tolstoy (1828–1910)

I N 1981, THE WORLD WATCHED IN WONDER AS THE SPACE
shuttle Columbia landed. At that time, it was the most advanced
vehicle built in human history, less than ninety years after the
Wright brothers first took flight in 1903. The world's imagination was
captured by space exploration. There were space camps for kids, and
movies were even made about the space camps. There was a national
energy about how exciting NASA was, and the organization was viewed
as the technological leader around the world.

NASA's culture at the time focused on drive—drive to hit deadlines,
to burn the midnight oil, and to take risks. Sadly, it was this culture
that many believe ultimately contributed to the Columbia's—and then
eventually the Challenger's—destruction.

There has been a great deal of analysis about how NASA went
from the pinnacle of scientific accomplishment in the thirty-year span
from the 1960s to the 1990s to falling from grace. NASA is no longer
the leader in the space of space. There are a number of different competitors today.

Research shows[33] how the culture at NASA began to evolve—how
the vernacular and terminology began to change, and how this culture
shift led to disaster. The issues with the space shuttles that caused them

---

[33] Mary R. Price and Teresa C. Williams, "When Doing Wrong Feels So Right: Normalization of
Deviance," *Journal of Patient Safety* 14, no. 1 (March 2018): 1–2, https://doi.org/10.1097/pts
.0000000000000157.

to blow up were not unknowns. The engineers had identified flaws—an O-ring in the Challenger and the foam in the Columbia—that they knew held the potential for catastrophe.

But the culture and focus of the organization drove them to continue to launch the shuttles anyway. In team meetings, an engineer raised the issue that erosion in the O-ring could occur during the flight. That erosion, he said, could create a malfunction. But the leaders were incentivized to hit deadlines and launch dates. In fact, engineers called out these flaws in recorded calls, and leaders in the organization responded, "But there's no risk to flight, correct?"

Incentive is an invisible force that shapes human behavior. When organizational leaders are putting pressure on the people who work for them—at NASA or anywhere else—and framing questions in ways that preclude the answers, it prevents transparency and dealing with the reality of the situation. In the flight-risk question, for instance, that leader gave the engineer very little choice outside of answering, "Correct."

Had that leader said something such as, "Tell me more," or, "What is the risk to flight?" they would have teased out a critical conversation that may very well have prevented the tragedies that followed.

## GET IT RIGHT

YOU MIGHT HAVE a strategy. You might have the best engineers on the planet. You might have grand plans of going to the moon and launching the most technologically advanced spacecraft in the history of mankind. None of that matters if you don't get the culture right. You must get to a place of egalitarianism, where people have the ability to raise their hands and call out issues without fear of punishment. Otherwise, you're not harnessing the collective wisdom of your resources. You're not utilizing the gifts you have before you.

Do you value creative tensions in your organization? Do you value the fact that no single person has all of the answers? Do you instill all of this through the values of your organization? If you do, you're likely moving in the right direction and will be wrong far less often. If you don't, you are setting yourself up for eventual failure as you are building in organizational blind spots. NASA built those blind spots in over the course of time. Their blind spots didn't just happen overnight—they occurred over the course of time, as the values influenced the culture. After all, culture is simply a series of beliefs and behaviors.

If you get your organizational values right, you get the culture right. If you get the culture right, you get the beliefs right. If you get the beliefs right, you get the behaviors right. If you get the behaviors right, your organization begins having better outcomes.

Whether it's in operational risk management or digital security risk management, you end up making better decisions that are better informed and that factor into multidisciplinary, diverse perspectives, which, in turn, lead to success.

## A TARGET ON THEIR BACK

THE SECURITY BREACH at a well-known retailer (Company Y) is a classic-use case that business schools are likely to study for years to come.

In a digital ecosystem, understand that, in addition to eventual targets, others are also susceptible to harm by being peripheral aspects of an invasion. You can think about it like this: when the United States fought in World War II, we didn't attack Japan first. We attacked the islands surrounding Japan in an island-hopping strategy that positioned us to attack Japan.

This is exactly what happened to Company Y.

The attackers did not go after Company Y itself. Instead, they compromised a vendor that Company Y trusted. It's harder to defend an attack from a trusted partner than someone from the outside world. Many organizations have the right walls in place, but they don't properly analyze the trusted relationships they might have. With Company Y, the attackers' end goal was to compromise millions of credit cards because they could resell those credit cards on the black market. To get that data, the attacker island-hopped off the back of Company Y's trusted vendor to break into their system.

As with other organizations, Company Y had the proper tools in place. They spent a great deal of money on people and technology. But their process had not evolved to challenge their own views of the world and to continuously validate their controls. You can buy the best armor in the world and you can hire all of the right people, but if you're not actually tuning your solutions for your environment, then you're going to miss critical items.

The technologies Company Y implemented kept flashing false positives. In this case, a false positive is an alert that says something bad is occurring, but when you go to respond, there's nothing actually happening. In Company Y's case, it was very much a boy-who-cried-wolf scenario. The people of the village got used to the normalization of risk deviance. The next time the system cried wolf, no one paid any mind—and the wolf killed the sheep and the boy. In the eyes of Company Y's analysts, it became normal to see a red alert and they didn't have a culture that challenged their own assertions and logic.

You might own a Stradivarius, but if you're not constantly tuning that instrument, you will not get beautiful music out of it. The same applies to your security staff. If you're not constantly tuning them, you're not going to get the outcome you want.

In this case, normalization of risk deviation ensued. Imagine if every time you came to a stoplight, it flashed red. You'd stop the first and second time, but if it stayed red all the time, you'd go past that stoplight. Likely, at some point, an accident would occur.

Company Y had the best of intentions. Their internal culture allowed for investing in the right technology and people, but it didn't allow for the self-awareness to challenge their own logic—to challenge how they configured their tools. That lapse *did* allow for normalization of risk deviance to set in. As a result, consumers were impacted across the country and maybe even the world.

Andy Grove, one of the co-founders of Intel, said that only the paranoid will survive. If you want to protect your organization in the digital age, you need to be paranoid. You need to have the attitude that the glass is half empty and ask how you can keep getting water in it. How do you enhance your controls? How do you ensure that you're challenging yourself to tune the tools?

In that spirit of continuous validation, you need to have a plan. The critical security controls we've highlighted throughout this book give you twenty key controls, broken down into 171 sub-controls across three tiers. You need to implement those 171 controls, validate them continuously, and test their inner and outer thresholds.

That means asking: what does normal traffic look like and what does the deviation from that mean both above and below? If you see a system that has a million connections a day on average suddenly drop to one thousand connections per day or jump to two million per day, you need to have monitoring in place to spot that deviation from the mean so you can understand what changed.

This is part of the philosophy of sophisticated continuous monitoring, and it should occur not just for your systems and applications, but for your culture and processes as well. You must have an eye out for complacency, thinking through the different permutations and complexities that can occur when you are managing an otherwise healthy environment.

## Critical Security Control 3:
## Continuous Vulnerability Management[34]

While we can perform continuous validation on technology and process, where you really need a gut check is when it comes to the continuous validation of your culture.

You start with values, beliefs, and behavior, which leads to your culture. The culture at NASA evolved to accept risks through various nomenclatures and putting pressure on individuals to say "yes"

---

[34] "CIS Control 7: Continuous Vulnerability Management." Center for Internet Security, accessed May 18, 2021, https://www.cisecurity.org/controls/continuous-vulnerability-management/.

even when it was not in anyone's best interest to do so.

An organization must identify what its values are and how it can attract the sort of people who resonate with those values to develop the culture it wants. In today's world, a healthy and enlightened business is one with a risk-aware mindset.

Your business needs to be aware of the external—and internal—risks facing it.

What is your intellectual property? What is the chance that insiders will want to get to it? Do you have the right culture in place for people to raise their hands and call out when they see something wrong? And how do you validate that culture exists? How do you let your people know you're listening? That you care?

Seek to understand—then to be understood. Make sure your culture establishes an environment in which people are both listening and feel free to speak. When that happens, every single person is part of your team, and they will all be on the lookout for the best interests of the organization. If you can foster that attitude, you're building the right culture, where people think of the company first, themselves second, and enhance the speed of trust throughout your business.

Create an environment where the mercenaries become missionaries, leading to a greater risk-aware mindset and culture.

## THE HUMAN ELEMENT

ANYONE WHO WANTS to protect their organization needs to understand human psychology to some degree.

In fact, if I were to bring together a group of subject matter experts to best defend a critical organization, I'd have security, privacy, operations, and statistical analytics experts, as well as a number of psychologists in the mix. We talk so much about the systems and applications, the technologies and processes, but we don't spend nearly enough time discussing the human elements and the psychology of risk. This is especially true when it comes to the normalization of risk deviation.

We've discussed in Chapter Seven the work of Kahneman and Tversky and the concept of the two systems in the brain. Security operators typically work an eight-hour day, but when they're working an incident, those eight hours can quickly turn into ten-, twelve-, and even twenty-hour days. I've worked war rooms that lasted all day and night. Without question, whether it's crisis management in the digital realm or managing miners that have been caught underground, the efficacy of decision-making degrades and fatigues you at the same time.

When we think about the decisions we're making (or what we as leaders are incentivizing our teams to decide), when it comes to defending our organizations and managing crises, we have to factor in that both mental and physical fatigue will set in. When someone stays up for twenty, thirty, or forty hours, they can fall into hero/victim/villain triangles.

You might be the hero today and come to someone's rescue—but you might overdo it. In the process of trying to be a hero, you might cause the very disaster you're trying to prevent. In running disaster recovery exercises, one of the key tenets is that when you're preparing for a disaster, do not cause the disaster for which you are preparing. This happened in the Love Canal incident that happened in Niagara Falls, New York, in the 1970s. The nuclear generator there began to have issues. The operators were tired and stressed. Due to human error, they caused the very nuclear fallout they were trying to prevent.

Understanding the pressures that individuals feel, whether internal or external, is crucial. Sophisticated attackers know to start by targeting a human being. That means attackers don't just compromise the system—they try to compromise the defenders who are protecting an organization, and they do that through various forms and functions.

In Operation Aurora, the employees of a well-known technology organization were targeted, but not through a simple spray-and-pray campaign or by exploiting a vulnerability. The attackers leveraged the social media accounts of friends of people who worked within that organization, submitting emails or social media requests through those friends.

The human element is perhaps the most important thing to consider when it comes not only to the normalization of risk deviation, but to the overall hygiene of your digital security environment.

## ESTABLISH AND MAINTAIN TRUST

THE EVOLUTION OF NASA's culture to focus on hitting deadlines above all else ultimately superseded their ability to speak candidly with one another. While short-term deadlines were met, this evolution contributed to massive errors and the gradual demise of the organization over the long term.

General Jim "Mad Dog" Mattis, sometimes called a "warrior monk," was not only a general in the United States Marine Corps, but also the secretary of defense and the author of *Call Sign Chaos*. He has a simple three-step approach to establishing and building trust in the Marine Corps, and it applies well to this topic. That approach is summarized in the three Cs. These are qualities you will want in the people you entrust to defend your organization.[35]

1. *Competence*: be technically and tactically competent. You know your job inside and out. Mattis tells us to be brilliant in the basics. Know your weaknesses and strengths. Work to improve yourself in every way: physically, emotionally, intellectually, and socially. All great leaders are balanced across many domains of ability. Anything that is not supporting your organization's main effort is of secondary importance.

2. *Caring*: when people know you are vested in their character development, their dreams, and their families, you are connected to their soul. Only in this way can you obtain their loyalty and devotion. Furthermore, if you care about your people, they will know it and you can speak to them bluntly when they disappoint. Show no favoritism, but value those people who make your organization tick.

3. *Conviction*: those who surround you (family, friends, and close peers) know what you stand for and also what you do *not* stand for. People who follow you catch on fast. State your rules and guidance in clear, certain terms and stick to them. Be sure to practice personal humility and compassion for those who follow. Only through deep conviction can you expect to win their hearts.

The three Cs develop an inner sensory alarm to the dynamics we describe at NASA and the corporate-speak that can sometimes

---

[35] Douglas R. Satterfield, "USMC Gen. Mattis: 3 Cs of Leadership," *The Leader Maker*, last modified September 19, 2019, https://www.theleadermaker.com/usmc-gen-mattis-3-cs-of-leadership/.

sugarcoat situations, create rosy pictures, and prevent us from dealing with reality, warts and all.

We want to have a sense of purpose and meaning in our lives. We want to have a voice and to have that voice be heard. That's just being human.

From an organizational perspective, the goal is to stay in the game. Maintaining relevancy should be one of the foundational components of your long-term brand strategy.

But how do you actually do that? How many organizations that were in the S&P 500 fifty years ago aren't around anymore? Where are the Kmarts, the Sears, the GEs, and the foundational blue-chip stocks of US corporate America back in the 2000s?

One of the hardest things for an organization to do is to stay relevant, not just as a leader but within the industry itself. As you think through your financial planning and results, as you think through the eyes of your customers and how you continuously serve them as appetites change (especially in today's rapidly fluid environment), you have to consider how you maintain trust with the companies and customers you provide for. Whether you are business-to-consumer or business-to-business, maintaining trust is a key component to your future relevance. The loss of that trust will erode your company's prosperity and, potentially, its existence.

You must think holistically. Most CEOs and business leaders think about financial numbers, market share, sales, profits, and losses. Start thinking about how well you are maintaining trust with your clients, employees, and the ecosystems you serve. How are you being a good steward of the information you possess? How are you protecting your organization and the environment that you participate in? How are you arming yourself and investing appropriately so that, as you build the next new piece of technology to serve your clients, you are factoring in the total cost of ownership and protection of that technology?

The enlightened organization will consider how to maintain trust through good security, privacy, and risk management practices. They'll also do so through transparency and frank conversations.

When there is a problem, be open to talking about the problem. What happened at NASA was because they began to lose that transparency through the very language they used. There was an almost implied sleight of hand, making communication opaque—and that lack of transparency led to tragedy.

Transparency goes hand in hand with trust. Be open and clear so that the little things don't create irreversible damage.

# CONCLUSION

## The Trojan War and the Greek Concepts of Bia[36] and Metis[37]

*Be still, my heart.*
*Thou hast known worse than this.*

—Homer (800–701 BC)

WE STARTED THIS book by talking about my childhood and how it felt to have a threat introduced into my family's home, a place I considered a safe environment, by outside forces beyond our control.

There was a moment in history that paralleled that experience, one that touches upon many of the concepts we've discussed throughout this book—the Trojan War. Most of us know the broad strokes of the story—but before getting into the premise, it is important to understand the ancient Greek concepts of *bia* and *metis*.

---

[36] "Bia (Mythology)." Wikipedia, accessed March 14, 2021, https://en.wikipedia.org/wiki/Bia_(mythology).

[37] "Metis (Mythology)," Wikipedia, accessed February 13, 2021, https://en.wikipedia.org/wiki/Metis_(mythology).

*Bia* was the essence of strength as a matter of force, captured in the character of Achilles. *Metis* was the essence of cunning, captured in the character of Odysseus.

Each attribute comes with its own associated balcony and basement. Achilles's strength and skill in battle was heralded in the ancient world, and his enemies feared him, which worked to his advantage. However, his balcony attribute of strength came with its own basement attribute (or blind spot) in the form his heel, which was susceptible to threats he ignored.

Odysseus, on the other hand, captured the essence of cunning with the balcony of agile thinking through new challenges, paired with the basement of people being wary of his reputation and having little trust in him. These characteristics required balance.

Homer captured these characteristics masterfully in *The Iliad*.

As the story goes, the Trojan War had gone on for ten years with the Greeks unable to break through the Trojan walls. So, they feigned weakness, as Napoleon also would much later with his "weak" flanks at the battle of Austerlitz. The Greeks left the battlefield in a false retreat and returned with a large hollow wooden statue, known forevermore as the Trojan horse. The horse was presented as a tribute to the Trojans in acknowledgment of their victory. The Trojans reveled in their victory and the gift appealed to their egos. They let their guard down, opened the gates to Troy, and pulled the horse inside.

The Trojans celebrated into the late hours. Once they were asleep, the Greek soldiers who had been hidden inside the horse slipped out, reopened the gates of Troy, and the Greek Army stormed in and slew almost every Trojan citizen.

As an interesting aside, two of the escapees, Romulus and Remus, fled to Italy and became the founders of Rome. Even in the destruction of Troy, the seeds of a future empire were sown.

What we learn from Homer's *Iliad* is that you can defend a city well for ten years, and in one night you can lose it all to a sneak attack.

Extrapolated out to the discussions in this book, we learn that you can defend a business well for ten years, and in one night you can lose it all to a cyberattack. You can think of yourself as immune to attack, only to have one weakness exploited. That's potentially all it takes for all that you hold dear to come crumbling down. You must have the ability to maintain two opposing thoughts in your head. Be pleased with your effort in this space and yet realize at the same time that more, much more, needs to be accomplished.

## ONLY RIGHT ONCE

WHEN IT COMES to your digital defense, it is not enough to only be strong. You must *also* be cunning.

Achilles was reputed to be the greatest warrior of the Greeks. Dipped as a baby into the River Styx by his mother, Thetis, Achilles was thought to be near invulnerable—except for his heel, where Thetis held Achilles as she submerged him in the water.

Achilles fought for many years with a sense of invulnerability—and hubris. It only took one poisoned arrow, expertly placed by Paris of Troy, to Achilles's unprotected heel to end his life and reign as one of the greatest soldiers the world had ever seen.

When it comes to digital risk management, the good guys (read: you) have to be right *all* the time. The bad guys only have to be right once.

It was not enough for Achilles to rely on his strength. It made him dangerously self-assured. Certainly so small an area on his body could not be exploited by his enemies—but it was, and at the cost of his life. Had he been cunning as well as strong, defensive as well as aggressive, he might have survived.

Where is the Achilles heel in your digital defenses?

## The Lion versus the Fox

Though often given a negative connotation, particularly in the Western world, it is just as important to be cunning as it is to be strong.

It's the eternal conundrum of the lion versus the fox.

Countless nature programs and articles are based around the lions in Africa leaving their pride to fight a battle against a pack of hyenas. The rest of the pride could come with the lion, but they don't. The lion is inherently strong and courageous. Sometimes he is victorious, but sometimes he isn't.

The lion's courage increases the probability of his death.

The fox is cunning in its survival techniques. It does not rush headlong into battle with its natural enemies. Foxes use deception and misdirection to avoid harm and to stalk their prey for food. As such, they've been characterized as sly. When a person is branded in the same fashion (sly as a fox), it's given a pejorative connotation, as if they are some sort of trickster.

And yet, the fox survives.

Odysseus employed cunning in fashioning the wooden horse to

enter the city undetected, resulting in ultimate victory for the Greeks. Their head-on assaults to the walls of Troy only saw them repelled again and again. It wasn't until they used deception and subversion that they were able to reduce their losses and win the war.

## FIND THE BALANCE

IN CYBER WAR, you must think to protect, detect, and correct, all of which must be orchestrated with a focus on traceability, accountability, and sound governance.

One of the ways organizations can be successful in this as they mature and evolve their protection controls is to practice deception. This practice is a true layer of defense as you walk up the maturity curve and another tool in your ever-growing toolbox. We know from the *Seven Habits* book that we must not only sharpen the saw—we need to know when and where to use it.

When you first start a company, when you've only got one or two people working, you're not investing time, money, and effort in deception—but there is a stack of technology that's been developing over the last decade that operationalizes deceptive layers of protection for businesses. For example, there are the honeypots to deceive malicious threat actors, as we discussed in Chapter Six. In addition, there are companies that create a virtual labyrinth (much like the King of Crete built the labyrinth to capture the powerful and threatening Minotaur).

A cunning use of digital deception convinces your attackers that they've been successful when they haven't. They are lured into your labyrinth, and while they waste their time attempting to work their way through it, you examine their behavior, tactics, and the software and tools they use so you can learn from their attack while nullifying the threat. You can then use this information to shore up your defenses.

Some malicious attackers will use Trojan software embedded in an email that appears to be, for example, from the CEO of your company. Because you believe it to be from your boss, you click on the link, and the horse breaches your walls. However, if your organization has a sandbox deception-layer environment, then the attacker will only gain a foothold within that environment—not on your internal network. They'll be stuck in the labyrinth. When do you spend time, money, and effort hardening your defenses? When do you invest the time to create a deceptive layer for your organizational controls?

One needs to balance both strength and cunning in order to manage a resilient program.

## AN ENDLESS JOURNEY

THE COMMON THREAD in fighting the 24/7 cyber war is to know thyself—and in the realm of digital defense, the journey to know thyself does not end.

If you ever feel content, if you feel like you've done enough, that you're satisfied with the layers of defense you've built for your organization, you must remember that the efficacy of controls degrades over time. Exceptions you bring into your risk profile will ossify your controls, making them more brittle and likely to break.

Remember: the road to hell is paved with risk exceptions; only the paranoid will survive.

You have to stay humble and hungry. You need to continuously search your environment. You need to expect that 20 percent of your people, processes, and technology are broken.

Learn from the Trojans, who snatched defeat from the jaws of victory by opening their gates because they assumed the Greeks were praising them. Their egos allowed them to believe that the horse was there to celebrate them rather than imperil them. That moment of self-adulation led to their downfall.

Don't let the same happen to you.

I hope this book instills in you a renewed feeling of self-awareness, a sense of curiosity, and an interest in developing a strategy as a sustained act where your future ideas adapt to the circumstances not just within the physical realm but in the digital realm as well.

## FAILING TO PLAN...

THE REVEREND DR. Martin Luther King, Jr. said:

*When evil men plot, good men must plan.*

About planning, the Prussian field marshal Helmuth von Moltke said:

*No plan survives first contact with the enemy.*

Finally, much later, while in the role of general during World War II, Dwight D. Eisenhower said:

*In preparing for battle, plans are useless,*
*but planning is indispensable.*

In linguistics, syncretism is "the merging of different inflectional varieties of a word during the development of a language." This is still Day Zero in the development of cyber risk management. Still, the amalgamation of various disciplines for overall resilience has begun; the integration of multi-disciplinary objectives for better business outcomes is on the next horizon for our industry. This work is going to be essential to your business strategic planning.

As you gain awareness of the digital threat landscape, begin to integrate your thoughts, views, and business planning with your risk tolerances in the digital domain. Understand that from the moment you close this book, you're now at the beginning of an ongoing journey of greater self-awareness, both for yourself and for your organization.

The planning doesn't end. The work doesn't stop.

Rather than having a beginning, middle, and end, your strategy must be an ever-adaptable plan with a story that enables you to navigate shifting sands. Like a chess game being played in an unending soap opera of ever-changing characters (both good and bad) and with scenarios and scenes previously unimaginable, your ability to adapt will be essential.

Plato once said, "Only the dead have seen the end of war." Sadly, in our world, only the dead have seen the end of cyber war.

I don't want that for you. I want our journey to continue together.

Let me hear from you.

Tell me how this book has altered your perspective as you prepare for cyber war in order to have cyber peace at nick@nickshevelyov.com.

# ACKNOWLEDGMENTS

AS I FINISH writing this book, I approach the ten-year anniversary of my father's passing. The retired marine raised his son on the values of the Marine Corps: honor, courage, and commitment. He lived an honorable life, showed courage in publishing an accurate map of Moscow while in the Soviet Union in direct disobedience of the KGB, and was committed to teaching his son the lessons of history, starting with a story about a Spartan boy that caught a fox and put his discipline and training ahead of his own self-interest. Those lessons are all as close to me today as they were then. They helped form the perspectives I have shared with you in this book.

When I was a teenaged boy, older than the Spartan child, I heard a strange noise in the night in the wooded area behind our house. I had the forethought to put on a pair of workman's gloves before going out to explore. As I pushed my way through the brush, something dashed out of the shadows, and I instinctively grabbed for it—and caught it.

It was a baby fox.

My father and I raised that fox together. We named him Shaloon
—Russian for rascal. Caring for that fox was one of the most meaningful
things we had ever done together as father and son.

In his final words to me, he said "Do not weep."

In these final words, a man who was once a boy honors his father
in memoriam.

Finally, I would like to thank my family, friends, and colleagues
for their support in writing this book. I would also like to recognize
the industry thought leaders whom I have learned from over the years,
several of whom have generously commented on this material.

Some companies and individuals mentioned in this book may be
or have been clients of my employer, Silicon Valley Bank.

# ABOUT THE AUTHOR

**NICK SHEVELYOV** is a specialist in cybersecurity, information technology, data privacy, and risk management with experience in multiple industries—from an engineering to executive and board advisory level.

A guest speaker at a variety of industry events, Nick has an undergraduate degree in economics, an executive MBA, and CISSP, CIPP, and CISM industry certifications.

Learn more at nickshevelyov.com.